Sewing for the Romantic Home

Volume One
Kitchens and Dining Rooms

To Sharon - enjoy & good luck on your B&B
Randi

Published by Classic Press
7700 Irvine Center Drive, Suite 800
Irvine, California 92618

Distributed by Classic Press
Proudly printed and bound in the USA

ISBN 10-9787127-0-6
ISBN 978-0-9787127-0-9

About the Author

Kandi Christian has always been creative.

Born as a native Californian, she was a child of 'The Sixties' and came to believe in her ability to do whatever she wanted to. The 70's saw her turn her love of sewing to teaching (for the Singer Company), before switching to the nascent computer industry and rising up to, then though, the glass ceiling - ending as a Vice President of a national computer company. All through-out those years, she never stopping experimenting with new sewing techniques and machines, and taught herself to design, as well as make, home decor and heirloom items. The 80's saw the growth of a family and the purchase of what would become a living prototype for the Romantic Home. It was also when Kandi's Cottage was born - another outlet for her creative energy. By the start of the 90's, Kandi was deeply involved in the world of haut couture, both as a designer and an enthusiastic consumer. She quickly became an early-adopter and exponent of machine embroidery and its design process, and started to create beautiful sewn items for her home. One of her final transformations was into the World of Heirloom Sewing - where she discovered, then perfected, sewing techniques from the reign of Queen Victoria.

As the new millennium dawned, Kandi finally put her life's experiences together and started a company teaching women from many countries Heirloom Sewing techniques using hand-on classroom methods. From classic heirloom items such as museum quality heirloom quilts to 'everyday' home décor items, she applies her unique insights and life-long passion to sewing for the romantic home.

Today, she still teaches all over the United States and overseas, and speaks at major sewing conferences such as Designs in Machine Embroidery and Women Create! She has worked as an expert seamstress on BBC Television productions and published articles in magazines such as Embroidery Journal and Designs in Machine Embroidery. Her future goals include continuing this series of books promoting Sewing for the Romantic Home. These books are carefully designed to guide everyone, from the everyday sewer to sewing expert, in the art, passion, and craft of creating items to enhance the home, however grand or humble, with gracious and romantic touches.

Nigel Blackwell
Royal County of Berkshire, England
May, Two-Thousand and Six

Projects List

From the moment you open this book you'll be able to start making these exquisite projects:

Project	Featured Technique
Hemstitched Pansy Towel*	Drawn-thread Hemstitching
Muted Flowers Madeira Towel*	Madeira Appliqué Hem
Victorian Monogram Lace Towel*	Lace Edging
Formal Monogram Napkins	Four-sided Hemstitching
Monogrammed Luncheon Napkins	Four-sided Lace Edging
Napkins for All Seasons	Drawn-thread Hemstitching
Windsor Placemats	Gimp Work and Lace Shaping
High Tea Table Runner	Reverse Madeira Appliqué
Elegant Lace Table Runner	Rayon Lace to Fabric
Sophisticated Runner Mats	Free-form Gimp Work
Delicate Table Topper	Lace Shaping and Lace-to-Fabric
Pretty Pot Holders	Lace-to-Fabric / Make with Scraps
Coasters with a Romantic Flair	Hemstitching / Make with Scraps
Rose and Lace Tiebacks	Fabric Roses / Make with Scraps
Folding Chair Covers	Scalloped Edges

*Instructions for turning these towels into a bottle carrier are included. Additionally, general guidelines for creating your own designs for towels, napkins, table covers and more are also provided.

Table of Contents

Before You Begin

Basic Techniques

Towels

Napkins and Table Covers

Make it from Scraps

It seems that I've been sewing all my life. Like so many people, I started sewing while I was young; sewing doll clothing, on a simple sewing machine that only sewed straight stitches. Later, in high school, the only way I could have as many nice clothes as I wanted was to make them *myself*. I soon realized that I could design and draft my *own* patterns for a unique look that no one else had. At that point came the transition from *sewing out of necessity* to *sewing for creativity*. The sheer joy and satisfaction that came from that creativity is the reason I sew to this day.

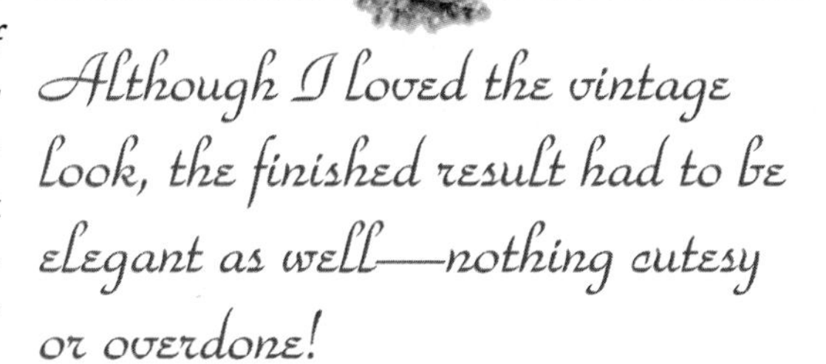

Many years later, I started sewing for my home. Sewing home décor is a very creative outlet. I discovered that I liked making unique home décor items that looked like they had been around for decades. I liked the vintage, romantic look of silk, linen and lace. I learned to shape lace and ribbon, loved to make pin-tucks, and created everything from table runners to pillow cases dripping with lace and added embroidery. Although I liked the vintage look, it *had* to be elegant as well—nothing cutesy or overdone!

Soon, my home, which was already furnished with antiques and collectibles, was filled with beautiful accessories that I'd created *myself* - like pillows, towels, sheets and table runners. I traded in my sewing machine for one that would embroider, and very soon I was adding monograms and embroidery to all my home decor. It gave my home the finishing touch needed to give it truly romantic accents.

Many years later, I read a book about heirloom sewing by Martha Pullen. I loved the book - so many things were similar to what I liked to sew. But, she had one technique I didn't understand at the time. It was about attaching entredeux to various fabrics and laces. But what in the world was this stuff called "*entredeux?*" I took off to my local fabric store. They didn't know what entredeux was either—other than to tell me it meant "between two" in French. So, I went to some other stores in our area—but no one had heard of *entredeux*. I re-read the directions and figured out what it looked like and how to use it from the drawings in the book. A few days later I was in a store in another state (I always visit fabric stores when I travel) and what should I find in their bargain bin? You guessed it - *entredeux*, for 15 cents a yard! I bought all that they had left, which was 20 yards of white and 30 yards of ecru. At the counter the clerk asked me why I would want that "ugly trim?" I told her it was used for heirloom sewing and was rewarded with a blank stare. I figured I shouldn't tell her what a great bargain I was getting or she might

change her mind. When I got home, I happily began experimenting with the entredeux and was soon adding it to my home decor projects.

I started giving my heirloom and vintage-style gifts to friends and family and it was not long before Kandi's Cottage was born. It is still in business today.

Kandi's Cottage is an Internet store filled with unique accessories for the home. But I wanted to do *more* in the field. I had once been a sewing instructor and decided to give it another try. I became a licensed Martha Pullen teacher and a freelance Husqvarna Viking educator. I began writing 'how-to' articles for magazines, and lecturing and teaching at trade shows.

All of this led to this book, which represents my passion for vintage sewing and for making beautiful home décor, and gifts for friends and family. I truly hope you enjoy reading it and making these beautiful projects as much as I do.

Here I am, doing what I love.

Kandi with Martha Pullen, graduating from Martha Pullen teacher licensing school.

I want to thank all the people who have helped make this book possible. Without them the book you now hold would have never have happened.

First of all, I want to thank Nigel Blackwell for putting up with all of the late nights and all of the crazy hours. He helped me with photo shoots, layout and most importantly, proof reading, editing and writing the "About the Author" section of this book.

I also thank him for helping me with my classes so I had time to write. He cut fabric and lace for kits, drove me to classes and helped make sure everyone in class was happy. He did such a good job that my students now look forward to the "distinguished Englishman" helping them to wind their bobbins, thread their needles, repeat the instructions, get them water and snacks, and most importantly admire their work. Nigel, thank you.

Thank you to Martha Pullen who encouraged me and said I could do it. You encouraged me and helped me with resources. This isn't the "dressed up sweatshirt" book we first talked about, but it is the book that I wanted to do first because it is a subject about which I have such passion. I will do the sweatshirt book sometime soon. Martha, you are such a sweet soul who brings joy to so many people by passing on your love of sewing. You are also so gracious. Thank you for letting me visit your home and wander through your wonderful attic filled with antique clothing. They are truly treasures.

Thank you Sue Hausmann; of Husqvarna Viking, for believing in me enough to hire me as an educator; what a wonderful time I had while I was "Keeping the World Sewing." I also loved having the opportunity to visit your lovely home too. You made me feel very welcome indeed.

And last, but not least, thank you to all of my students in this country and overseas, to whom teaching is such a joy. I get back from you so much more than I could ever give you.

Sue Hausmann with Kandi

Here are a few thoughts and ideas that will get you started. The next few pages will give you ideas for gift giving, introduce you to fabrics and laces, and tell you about the notions and supplies you will need.

Let's get started . . .

The projects in this book may *look* like they took days or even weeks to finish, but that's the real beauty of them. They are easy, easy, easy. If you can sew a straight stitch and a zigzag, you can create all the projects in this book. But shush - don't tell anyone, that's our secret!

The projects in this book may look complicated, however they are easy, easy easy, but shush – don't tell anyone, that's our secret!

Before we get to the projects, we are going spend the first half of the book covering some of the fundamentals of sewing for the romantic home: the colors, the fabrics and many tricks, tips and products that will make your life easier and your projects successful.

There is also a section called "Basic Techniques" that covers the special sewing techniques used for the projects in this book. This section will become a valuable reference later when you begin creating your own designs. You can just look up the appropriate techniques and review them before starting your project. If you have never tried a particular technique covered in the basics section, follow the instructions in that section and practice the method using fabric scraps. Then when you get to your project, you will be familiar with the procedure.

Throughout this book there are pictures of samples to inspire you. After you finish one of the book's projects, these samples will then give you ideas for creating your own masterpiece.

There is a list of sources at the end of this book from which you can purchase the fabrics, laces and notions used in the projects if you can't find them at your local fabric store. Also, the Internet is a great resource for supplies. Just type in what you are looking for into a search engine and voilà: thousands of Internet stores.

Look for this spool. It indicates a special tip to help make your sewing easier.

You may also order a kit for each project. These kits come with everything you need to complete the project:: the fabric, needles, stabilizer, lace, and thread. See the Supply Sources section on page 67 or the order form on page 93 for more information about ordering kits.

No matter how elaborate or humble the gift, presentation can always make it *much* better. If you are making one of the projects in this book for a gift, here are a few suggestions to make it even *more* special.

Before folding the item, lightly spray a piece of tissue paper with perfume, let it dry and place the tissue paper on the inside of the item. Fold the fabric so that you capture the tissue paper inside. When the recipient picks up the item, it will be a gift for all the senses: sight, touch, smell and sound.

Tie the gift with beautiful ribbon, lace and trim; then, just before you give it, add a few stems of fresh flowers as a finishing touch. Even a humble brown paper bag will look elegant when tied with beautiful ribbon and flowers.

Wrap the gift in a beautiful paper. Take a second coordinating paper and wrap it around the center of the box for a double-layered look. Now add your ribbon and bows.

A simple brown bag becomes something special when you add fresh flowers and a pretty tag. See the next page for directions to add these flowers so they keep fresh all day.

For this gift bag, we used lavender and sweet peas for their scent and color and added a touch of lobelia for an extra punch of color.

Fold three layers of a wet piece of paper towel into a small rectangle, about 1 x 3 inches, and lay it on a piece of foil. Lay the flowers on the paper towel with their stems on the towel - some will be facing up and others down.

The stems should be freshly cut to keep the flowers at their best. Fold the towel over the stem ends.

Tear the foil and tightly cover the paper towel. Tear off all the excess foil that you don't need.

Cover the foil completely with a piece ribbon so no foil shows. Place the flowers on the bag and tie a bow around it, use the photo on the previous page as a guide.

When teaching, I jokingly tell my students that there are only three colors in creating romantic home décor: white, off-white and off-off white (ecru). It sometimes seems that way, but actually, *any* colors may be used. Romantic colors don't **shout**, they *whisper*. You will find throughout this book mostly white and soft muted antique-looking colors—as they are still my colors of choice for accents. But I also love rich tones in my home décor. I like a navy couch with a beautiful off-white throw and linen and lace pillows on it. I love to add a touch of white upon a burgundy and chocolate brown bedspread that is adorned with gold bullion fringe.

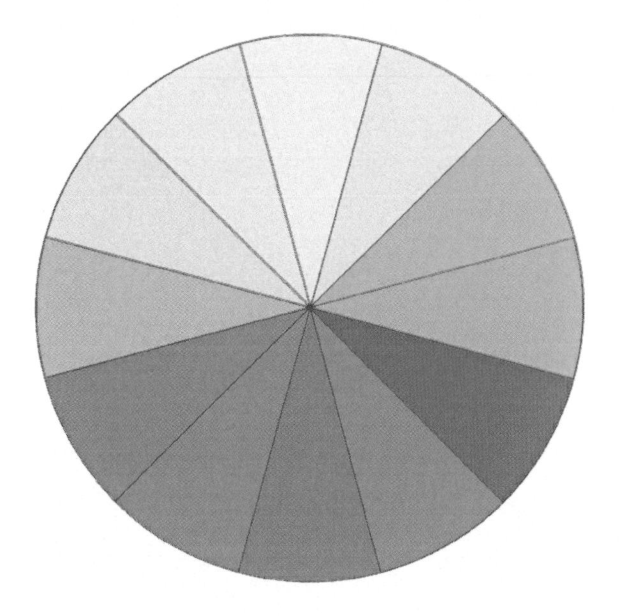

Despite evidence to the contrary, you *can* sew romantic home décor with bold colors, it's just that white and soft colors immediately say "romance".

Throughout this book the colors for the projects are listed as pictured, but feel free to change anything. If your tastes lean more toward country, feel free to use red, white, blue, black or yellow. If you prefer period, or Victorian, then emphasize claret, burgundy, rust and deep colors - or whatever suits you. Use this book as a starting point to indulge *your* creativity.

If making a gift, use colors to match the lucky recipient's own décor. If making something for someone whose house you've never been to before, use taupe, ecru and muted colors that give the appearance that the items have been around forever. Something that *looks* antique always fits into any décor, even modern.

*Romantic colors don't **shout**, they whisper.*

The look of a romantic home is a look that is truly timeless. When you create the projects in this book, you will want them to be around for generations to be heirlooms for your children and grandchildren. We therefore use natural fabrics for all the projects in this book.

We know from experience that natural fibers will last for hundreds, possibly *thousands*, of years. Natural fibers have been found in the tombs of Egyptian kings. We don't know yet if polyester or other man-made fabrics will last forever. Also, natural fibers add a luxury feel for very little cost. When you make something yourself, you can splurge on the fabrics and *still* make something that costs less than ready-made. Bask in the luxury of 100 percent cotton, linen or the best of all: silk. Whenever possible, purchase the best you can afford and use natural fibers; after all, the haute designers and top fashion houses do.

Natural fibers feel better and have more 'give' than man-made fibers. For some techniques such as machine hem-stitching, lace shaping and drawn-thread work, natural fibers are essential. While you can make many of the projects in this book with poly-blends, you will be *much* happier with your results if you use natural fibers and laces. Some techniques, such as lace shaping, simply can't be done with polyester or nylon laces.

All these bolts of fabric are in the colors of white, off-white and ecru, a classic look that is never boring if you vary the textures. If you prefer bright colors, feel free to use them instead of the colors shown in the projects.

The fabrics listed here are the ones used to create the projects in this book. Natural fibers are preferred because they give the best results. After all, if you are going to put in the time and effort to create something beautiful, then use the best fabrics you can afford.

There are times when you may want to use blends for a project, but this should be done only after you are familiar with the techniques and can tell when you are achieving the proper effect when using a blend. One of the beauties of polyester is that, although it is not so grand on its own, it generally takes on the characteristics of the other fiber when blended – if there is enough of the other fabric in the blend.

Linen

If silk is the Queen of fabrics, then linen is King. Throughout this book we use 100 percent linen, either lightweight (handkerchief) or medium-to-heavy weight. Linen is easy to care for, can be laundered repeatedly and yet still looks and feels wonderful. Linen has a nubby texture because it has threads of varying sizes.

The *weight* of the linen is described by the number of ounces per yard. For example, handkerchief linen is usually 3½ ounces per yard or less, medium-weight linen is around 4-6 ounces per yard and heavy-weight linen is 7 or more ounces per yard.

Rayon

If you can't find, or afford, 100 percent linen, then look for a blend made with Rayon. Unlike most man-made fibers, Rayon is not synthetic; surprisingly it's made from wood pulp! This fiber was first manufactured in the 1890's in France. Rayon's properties are closer to those of natural cotton or linen than to other manufactured fibers.

Batiste

Another fabric used in this book is batiste. Batiste is a lightweight smooth-textured cotton fabric that is often used in christening gowns, nightgowns and children's clothing. It comes in several weights and hands — all with different names and countries of origin. We used a delicate Swiss Nelona batiste for the Delicate Table Topper project. Tea towels made in batiste and edged with cotton lace are simply gorgeous.

When I first was introduced to cotton lace I thought it was so "flimsy" compared to the polyester lace I had previously used. It took time for me to learn to appreciate the beauty and quality of this delicate lace.

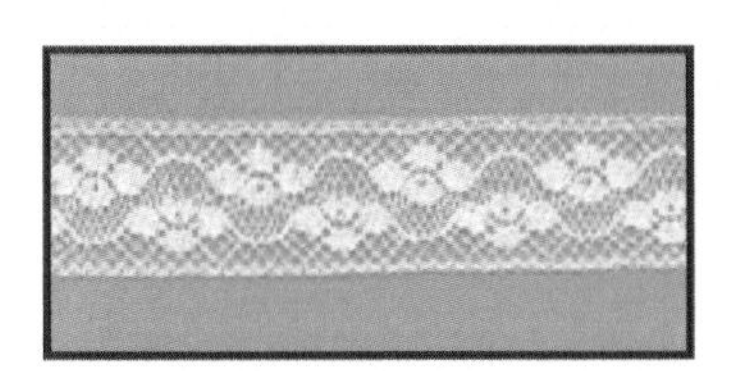

Cotton Insertion Lace

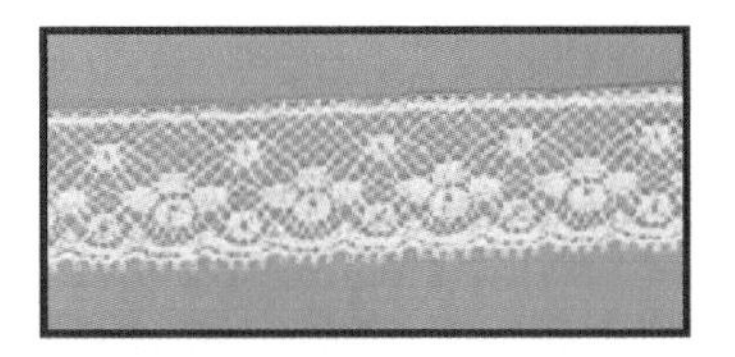

Cotton Edging Lace

Cotton Lace

When shaping lace, it is imperative that you use 100 percent cotton lace. Cotton laces are generally manufactured in France or England. Polyester or nylon laces will *not* shape properly because they do *not* have enough give. Also, they do not have a header thread to pull to create the shapes. Avoid them.

There are two types of cotton lace: *insertion* and *edging*. Insertion lace has multiple header threads on both sides and is used to insert between two pieces of fabric. Edging lace has header threads only on one side and has a decorative finish on the other side.

Rayon Edging Lace

Rayon Lace

For the Elegant Lace Towel (featured on the front cover) Rayon Venetian lace was used. This lace was sewn on the fabric flat rather than being shaped. It can be mitered around corners, but it cannot be shaped around corners. But because it is Rayon, you'll still get beautiful results that are just not possible with polyester laces.

The price of cotton lace is based on the complexity of the pattern. You can find the right width for your project in a variety of price ranges.

You don't need very many sewing supplies to create the projects in this book. You probably have most of them, such as a sewing machine, scissors and needles already. However, if you don't, your local fabric store, sewing machine dealer or the Internet are probably the best places to shop for supplies.

There is a reference section at the end of the book with sources for most of the supplies you may need.

Sewing Machines

The instructions in this book are suitable for *any* modern sewing machine. Almost all sewing machines manufactured over the last 25 years have a zigzag stitch, a reinforced stitch and at least a few decorative stitches. Although the specialty stitches that come with the top-of-the-line machines are wonderful, they are *not* required to create beautiful home décor. Drag out that sewing machine that has been sitting in your closet for the last 10 years—you'll be surprised what you can do with it! If you want a newer sewing machine, then sewing magazines and your local sewing machine dealer are the best place to learn about the various types of sewing machines available on the market today.

Embroidery Machines

If you are fortunate enough to have an embroidery unit for your sewing machine, the Compact Disk (CD) that comes with this book contains most of the embroidery designs shown in the samples. These designs are provided in formats suitable for almost all home embroidery machines. If you don't yet have a sewing machine with an embroidery unit, there are literally hundreds of pre-embroidered designs available in your local fabric store that can be stitched on to your project.

Sergers

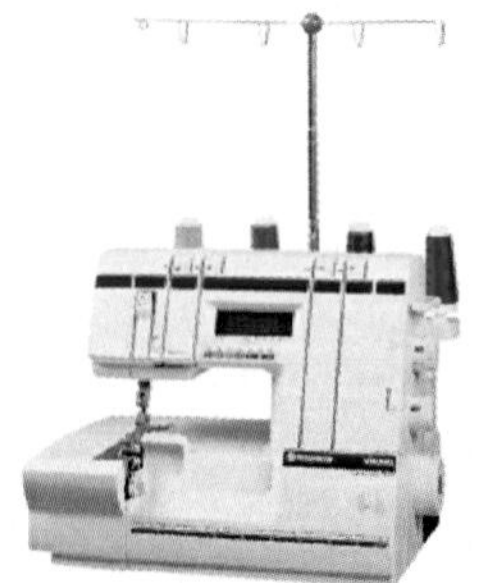

A serger, also called an overlock machine, is a great time saver. However, it is optional and instructions for construction techniques for both conventional sewing machines and sergers are included in each section. I only purchased my serger a few years ago. I now wonder what took me so long?! Although I have successfully sewn for years without one, my serger certainly makes sewing home décor easier and faster.

Needles

Each project's instructions include the recommended needle sizes.

Many of the needles used in the projects are large sizes, or they are *wing needles*. These create holes in the fabric as you sew. These holes are held open by a stitch that goes in-and-out of the hole more than once. If you have never sewn decorative stitches with a wing needle before, then you will be completely surprised by the results you get!

Back when I was a young girl sewing, a needle was never changed unless it broke. It was always a big deal to have to change the needle. It is a good thing that we used to sew over our pins and thus broke our needles often—or else we would never have changed them! Thank goodness that changing needles is the norm now. We now know that you should change your sewing machine needle after about 8 hours of sewing and, *never* sew over pins (no sewing machine manufacturer recommends sewing over pins!). The best rule of thumb for changing your needle is to put in a new one for each new project you start. Many times when it seems that your sewing machine is "acting up," it really *is* just a dull needle causing the problem.

When I'm in the middle of a project and am using several needles, I have a place in my sewing machine tray to hold them. I have marked this with the various sizes I use. If you don't have something like this, then a good way to keep track of your needles is to mark up a spare pin tomato with a different number in each section. Otherwise, it is wise to keep a high-powered magnifying glass in your sewing kit. Those numbers on the side of the needles are extremely small and almost impossible to read without magnification.

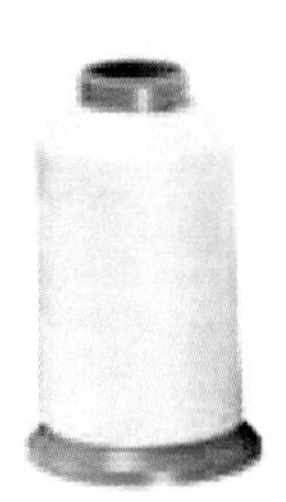

Thread

If you are making projects using natural fibers, it is best to use natural threads as well. Most of the projects in this book call for 60 weight cotton thread for construction. Additionally, when creating projects that use wing needles or large top stitching needles, lightweight cotton thread will help hold the holes open. Your embroidery thread should be either cotton or Rayon. Cotton embroidery thread gives a look closer to hand-work, while Rayon thread adds extra sheen to your project.

It is *very* important to use the correct size needle to obtain the desired result.

Wash-Away Basting Thread

One of those modern miracles that we have available to us today is a very important type of thread called *wash-away basting thread*. This wonderful product allows us to easily create Madeira appliqué without burning fingers with the iron trying to turn-under tiny seams. You will find this miraculous product useful for many projects and I will show you how.

Stabilizers

One of the biggest areas that separates merely "home-made" from "hand-crafted" is the use of *stabilizer*. It is often an overlooked or forgotten element. Beginners and experienced sewers alike sometimes leave out the stabilizer when sewing pin stitches or decorative stitches. The result will be pulled and distorted stitches and hems. In addition, once the item is washed, it will pucker at the stitch line if you don't use stabilizer.

What separates "home-made" from "hand-crafted" is the use of stabilizer.

Each project in this book recommends stabilizers for the techniques where it is appropriate. Take the time to include the stabilizer where it is specified in the directions. You will never regret using stabilizer when it's called for, but will *always* regret *not* using it.

Temporary Spray Adhesive

Another of the bona-fide modern-day sewing miracles we have at our disposal today is this wonderful product. It not only saves time, it allows easy *perfect* placement of lace and appliqués. Temporary spray adhesive holds things tighter and better than pins. It then just disappears into thin air after a while, leaving no residue.

Double Stick Fusible Tape

Double stick fusible tape, lets you position and re-position hems. Once you are happy, you just iron them down for a permanent bond. Be sure to follow the manufacturer's instructions for fusing. Also, read the product's label to make sure you can sew on the product after it is bonded.

Wash-Away Markers

With wash-away markers, once you wet the fabric, the markings disappear. Use plain water, not soap or bleach to remove the markings. These markers are blue in color and the ones that look like a marking pen are preferable to the ones that look like a pencil.

Once mastered, these basic construction techniques become the basis for all kitchen and dining linens. The only real difference between a table cloth and a placemat is size; the techniques used are the same.

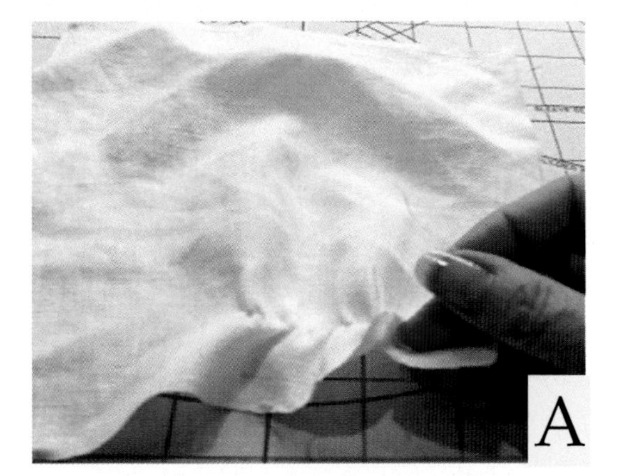

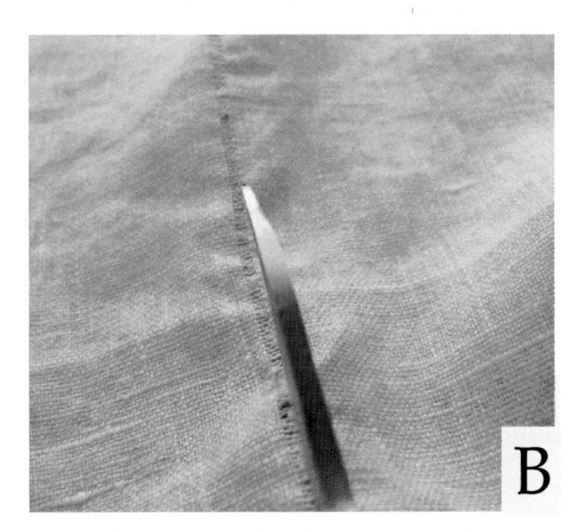

Prior to using linen, it should be washed. Since linen ravels easily, it is best to serge the edges prior to washing. If you don't have a serger, zigzag each raw edge.

When you cut a piece of linen, you need to make sure your linen is straight on grain. To do this you will need to pull a thread.

1 At the edge of the fabric make a small clip through the selvage edge about ½ an inch into the fabric.
2. Pull a thread loose from the others. This thread should go across the fabric perpendicular to the selvage edge.
3. Gently pull this thread, gathering the fabric slightly until you have a gather at the opposite selvage edge (as shown in photo A).
4. Clip into this opposite selvage edge cutting the thread that you pulled.
5. Pull the thread out from the fabric. This will create a line across the fabric for you to follow with your scissors (as shown in photo B).
6. Cut along this line and you'll have a cut that is perfectly on the grain line.

Washing Fabric

You can wash and dry linens just like any other fabrics. To keep linen looking its best without having to press it, take it out of the dryer while it is still slightly damp. Lay it flat on top of the dryer and smooth out the wrinkles with your hands. Let it dry in place. It will dry flat, smooth and crisp and ready to sew.

Rayon may be washed in warm water and dried using a "knit" setting. Use a very cool iron to press it.

Wash batiste in warm water and tumble dry on cool until it is almost dry. Remove it from the dryer and press it to remove the wrinkles.

Washing Lace

If the item you are washing has cotton lace attached to it, you can wash it using the same method as your cloth, but use a gentle cycle for your washing machine. If the lace is Rayon, wash and dry it on your gentle settings.

Ironing

Napkins, placemats and table runners look their best when they are ironed. If you don't have the time (or inclination) to iron them, just send them to be laundered. Be sure you ask you cleaners to *launder* your items, not *dry clean* them!

If you iron the items yourself, press them with the embroidery or monogram face down on a terry towel. This will keep the embroidery from being flattened by the hot iron. Adding a little spray starch not only makes ironing a little easier, it makes the item feel better to the hand.

Cotton lace can be ironed with a cotton setting using starch, but Rayon lace should be pressed using a Rayon setting. You may need to iron the cloth right up to the edge and press the Rayon lace separately. Alternatively, you can use a pressing cloth on the Rayon lace.

One note about ironing linens. If you are not planning to use them for a while, it is better to put them away flat or on fabric rolls so they don't get permanent folds and weaken the fibers.

Before using your fabrics, pre-wash or starch them and *then* iron them. You wouldn't want your projects to shrink after the first washing!

One of the more exciting aspects of sewing for the kitchen and dining room is that it is so easy to completely change the appearance of an item just by changing the hemming option.

You can change a design from "sophisticated" to "feminine" just by changing the hem. Once you master a hemming technique, you can use it for towels, napkins, placemats, table runners, table cloths or on any other project you wish.

All of the projects in the book can be made with a variety of hems. One of the most prominent and beautiful hems is a *hemstitched* edge. It is a hem that has tiny pulled holes at the hemline. This traditional finish is reminiscent of grand old hotels and luxurious ocean liners.

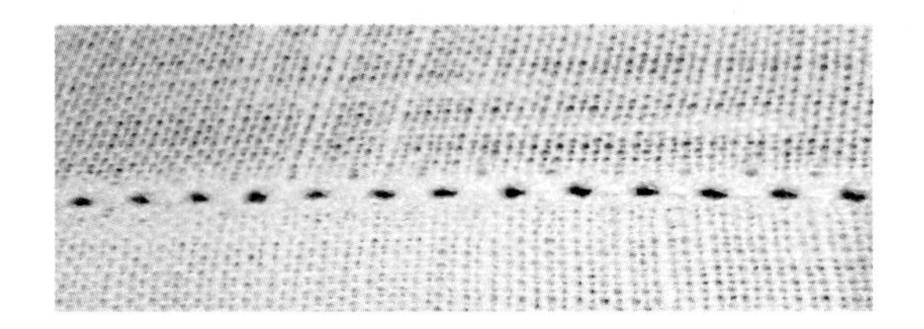

A hemstitched edge has tiny holes along the hemline.

Hundreds of years ago, hemstitching was done by hand and took weeks to complete. During Victorian times, hemstitching machines became popular. They were used to create hems with holes and were used in women's and children's clothing as well as for home linens. Today, hemstitching is done with a wing needle and a stitch that repeats back over itself more than one time. Most modern sewing machines have one or both of the hemstitches shown on page 18. If not, a reinforced straight stitch (one that goes back and forth over itself a couple of times) can be used at the hem line to duplicate the look.

Lace edges give your project a feminine touch.

A second and almost perhaps the easiest form of hemming, is a *lace-edged* hem. Lace-edged hems are more feminine than other hems. Lace is applied to the edges of towels and is mitered around the corners for napkins and table cloths.

Another edge that is both decorative and practical is a *scalloped edge*. If your sewing machine comes with a decorative scalloped stitch, this edge is quick and easy. Later in this book you will discover the secrets for creating perfect scalloped corners.

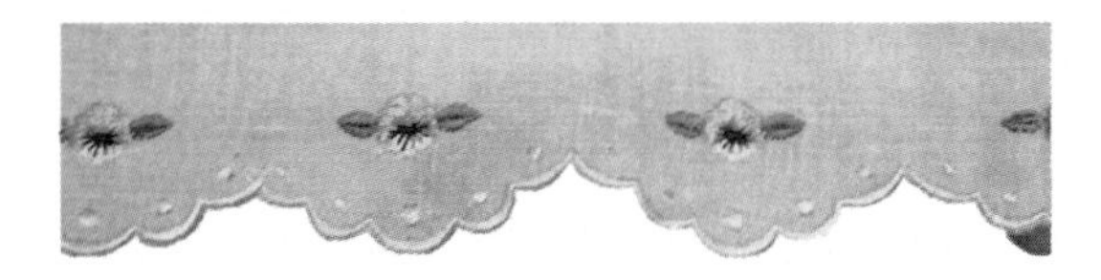

Today's sewing machines come with a variety of scallops.

The last hemming technique used in this book is known as a *Madeira appliqué hem*. Madeira appliqué is a technique in which a second piece of fabric is attached to the main fabric and is then pin-stitched along the edge. Any of the stitches shown here could be used to attach the appliqué, or the same effect may be created using a zigzag stitch to hold the appliqué down with a reinforced straight stitch sewn above the appliqué to simulate the look.

This fabric applied scallop is a Madeira appliqué.

Of course, you can always hem with the conventional "turned under twice and stitched" hem, but where's the fun in that?

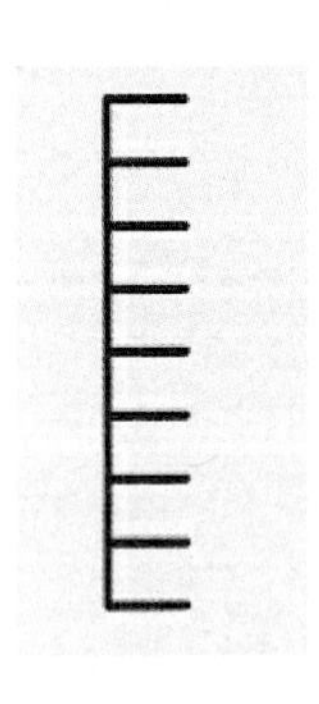

Pin Stitch

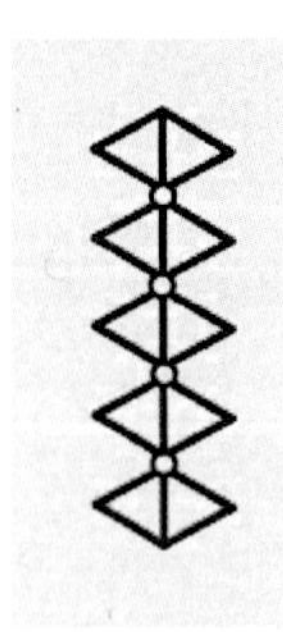

Entredeux Stitch

The perfect mitered corner isn't hard to do once you know the "trick" to making them. Like anything else, all it takes is a little practice.

Follow these instructions step-by-step and you'll find it so easy that, you'll wonder why you ever thought it was difficult.

1. Fold and press your hemlines above the fabric edges as shown in the top diagram.
2. At each corner, fold the two fabric edges together so the two hem fold lines from each side of the fabric match. You will have the item folded at a diagonal. (see A, B, & C below).
3. Draw a line at a 45 degree angle from the edge to the point where the hemline folds intersect. Sew along this line. (See D).
4. Trim off the extra fabric from the point next to the newly sewn seam and turn the corner inside out.
5. Press the item again and fuse the hem with double stick fusible tape to hold it in place.
6. Finish the hem according to the project directions.

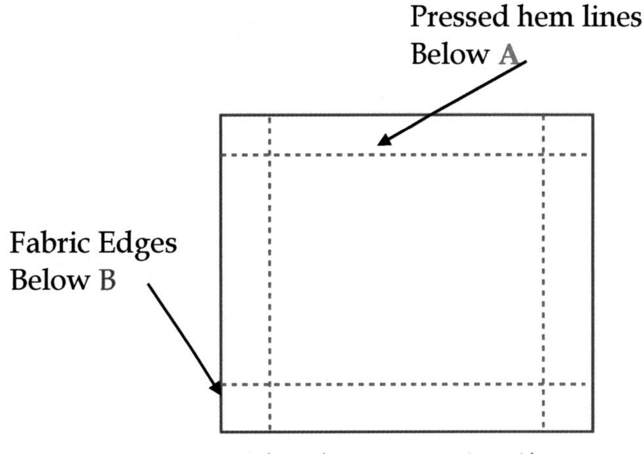

Fold and press your hemlines.

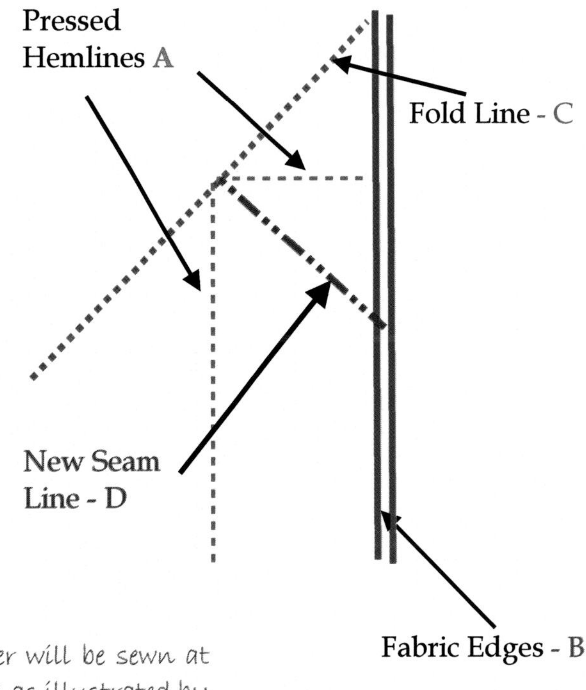

Each corner will be sewn at a diagonal as illustrated by the red line (see D above).

The picture above is the mitered corner from the right side. Notice how it's difficult to tell the difference between the right side above and the wrong side below. *That's* the perfect mitered corner.

Tiny holes along the hemline are the hallmark of fine linens both from days-gone-by and in today's top hotels and restaurants.

(above top) A close up of a hemstitched edge. Use it in towels (center) or at the end of a table runner (bottom).

This is the finish you will find on vintage linens from fine hotels. If you find this finish on new linens, the cost is generally very high. This hemming option allows you to add a sophisticated look to anything you create—at almost no additional cost.

1. If you have a serger then serge the edges of the towel, napkin, or placemat with a 4-thread overlock. If you do not have a serger then simply zigzag or overcast the edges.
2. Measure up from the edge you are hemming twice the finished hem size. For example, if you are creating a 1½ inch hem, measure 3 inches from the edge and make a line all the way across the fabric parallel to the edge with a wash-away marker. If you are making something with four sides, repeat this for each side.
3. Using a pin, pull out three rows of threads along the line you just made. If you are making a towel, then pull the threads all the way from one end of the fabric to the other. If you are making a 4-sided project, then only pull the threads up to the corner where the lines you drew intersect.

4. Fold over the hem to one thread below the pulled rows and press in place.
5. If you are making a towel, continue on from the next step. If you are making a 4-sided item, follow the instructions for mitering the corners on page 19.
6. Place strips of tear-away stabilizer under the hemline.
7. Use a pin stitch, entredux stitch, or one of your choice, to stitch the hem. Choose one that you like by testing stitches on a small scrap of linen in which you have pulled threads and turned under a tiny hem.

Napkins (top) and towels have a clean finished look when hemstitching is added.

8. If you are using a pin stitch, the teeth of the pin stitch should go into the hem area and the straight part of the stitch should run along the edge of the hem. If you are using another stitch to decorate, such as an entredeux stitch, then make sure you catch the hem in the side part of the stitch.
9. If you don't have a pin stitch, entredeux or another decorative stitch, you can simulate one by using a zigzag and a reinforced straight stitch. First, use a small zigzag stitch (L=1.5, W=1.5) to sew the hem into place. Next, run the reinforced straight stitch along the line created by the pulled threads. Make sure the forward and backward motion of the stitch is in the pulled thread area.
10. If the stitch you are using has a side-to-side motion, make sure you catch the hem in the side part of the stitch.
11. Tear away the stabilizer and press.

Towels like these make wonderful hostess gifts. They last much longer than flowers or wine. Make them to match the decor or taste of the recipient.

Of all the hemming options in this book, nothing says "romance" quite like the lace-edged hem. The wider the lace, the more delicate the piece looks. The technique is simple, but the result is *stunning*.

There are two methods of attaching lace depending upon whether the lace is cotton (see page 25) or Rayon (see page 26).

There is nothing lovelier and more romantic than lace-edged linens.

Method One—Cotton Lace

1. Use the technique for attaching lace to flat fabric explained on page 37.
2. If you are creating a towel, start with step 14.
3. To create the mitered corners, cut 4 pieces of lace that are the size of the item you are sewing plus 1½ times the width of the lace as overhang.
4. Start sewing the first piece of lace 1/8 inch from the corner, keeping the overhang you measured in step 3 extended beyond both edges (see photo A on page 26).
5. Sew to 1/8 inch from the next corner, once again extending the lace.
6. Start a new piece of lace for the next side remembering to extend the lace over the edge. Begin sewing 1/8 inch from the corner.
7. Continue for all 4 sides.
8. After you have attached the lace, you will need to miter each corner by folding one extended piece of lace at a diagonal over the other extended piece creating a 45 degree angle at the corner. Pin if necessary (see photo B on the next page).

A pretty lace edge can enhance the look of, and add romance to any napkin, placemat or table cloth.

9. Sew the two pieces together along the diagonal line created in step 8.
10. Press the lace to one side of the seam.
11. Use a small zigzag stitch (L=1.5, W=1.0) on the front of the lace from the fabric to the outside edge of the lace thus reinforcing the seam.
12. Cut off the excess lace as close as possible to the zigzag stitching.
13. Repeat this process for all four corners.
14. Using a wing needle, or a large topstitching needle, set the lace down with a pin stitch or entredeux stitch. If sewing a towel, sew across the lace, otherwise you will sew all the way around the four sides of the item.

    If you are using a pin stitch, the straight part of the stitch should be on the fabric and the "teeth" part of the stitch should go into the lace.

    If you do not have either stitch, use a size 75 needle to sew a small zigzag stitch (L=2.0, W=2.5) with the zig going into the fabric and the zag into the lace. Then sew a reinforced straight stitch along the fabric where it joins the lace with your wing needle or topstitching needle.

Method Two—Rayon Lace

1. Measure ½ inch above the raw hem edge and draw an line with your wash-away marker.
2. Spray along the line with temporary spray adhesive.
3. Lay the lace onto the line.
4. If you are creating a towel, continue from step 10.
5. To create the mitered corners, cut 4 pieces of lace that will extend 1½ times the width of the lace beyond the fabric corners.
6. Place a pin at each corner where the lace lays over the fabric.
7. Fold the lace over itself to create a 45 degree miter.
8. Pin the miter and continue in the same manner around all 4 sides.
9. On the last side, fold the lace under to create the miter.
10. Attach the lace to the fabric with a small zigzag stitch (L=1.5, W=1.5).
11. If sewing a towel, go to step 17.
12. Sew along the miter lines using the same small zigzag stitch.
13. Press the lace to one side of the seam.
14. Use a small zigzag stitch (L=1.5, W=1.0) on the front of the lace from the fabric to the outside edge of the lace to reinforce the seam.
15. Cut off the excess lace.
16. Repeat this process for all four sides.
17. Using a wing needle or a large topstitching needle, set the lace down with a pin stitch or entredeux stitch. If sewing a towel, sew across the lace, otherwise you will sew all the way around the four sides of the item.

    If you are using a pin stitch, the straight part of the stitch should be on the fabric and the "teeth" part of the stitch should go into the lace.

    If you do not have either stitch, use a size 75 needle to sew a small zigzag stitch (L=2.0, W=2.5) with the zig going into the fabric and the zag into the lace. Then sew a reinforced straight stitch along the fabric where it joins the lace with your wing needle or topstitching needle.

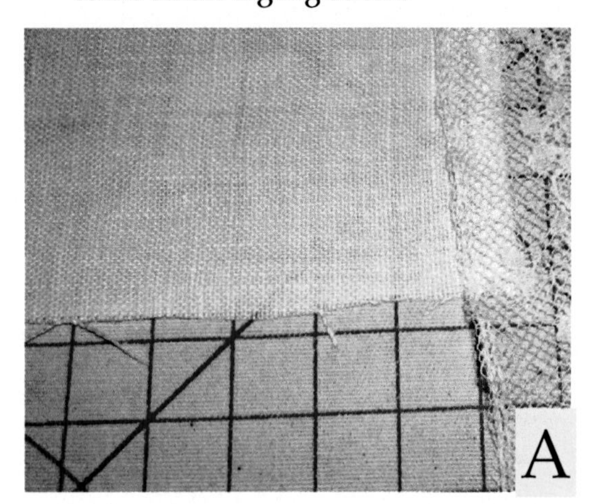

The lace should extend beyond the edge of the item to which you are attaching the lace.

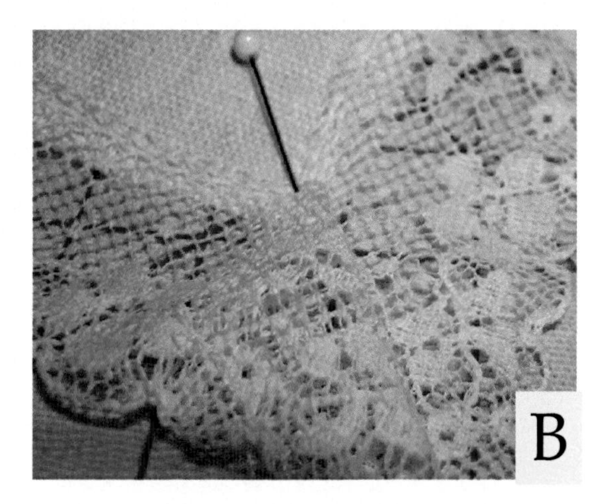

Whether using cotton or Rayon lace, miter the corners and pin in place before sewing the miter down.

A machine-scalloped hem is perhaps the easiest finish for your edges — the machine does all the work.

Today's modern sewing machines usually offer several different scallop options. Some machines have scallops that are over two inches wide. Scalloped edges look complex, but the sewing machine does all the work. All you have to do is follow a line as you sew.

1. Draw a hem line about 1 inch from the edge of the item with a wash-away blue marker. If you are using a large scallop, mark the hem line up from the edge the size of the scallop plus ¼ inch.
2. If you are making a towel, just mark the front and back hems straight across.
3. If you are making a napkin, tablecloth or any item with four sides, you will need to round the corners giving them a curve that is at least as large as one scallop. Use a coin or small glass to draw your corners (see below).
4. Place strips of tear-away stabilizer under the hem area.
5. Choose a scallop from your sewing machine that you find pleasing.
6. Sew the scallop design along the straight edge of the item.

An open toe foot allows you to see the cording as you sew.

Notice the cording is held in the special gimp foot as you sew.

7. If you are rounding corners, stop at the end of the scallop design just before the corner line starts to curve. Turn the corner and sew another single scallop. Do not try to turn the fabric while the machine is sewing, this will distort the scallop.
8. Finally, turn fully to the straight area and continue sewing the scallops.
10. Tear away the stabilizer.
11. Dab Fray Check™ or a similar liquid seam sealant product at the edge where the fabric meets the scallop. Do not soak the scallops, just lightly wet them. Let dry.
12. Trim the excess fabric away from the scallop as close to the stitches as possible without cutting the stitches.
13. As an optional advanced technique, use gimp cording and a tight satin or zigzag stitch (L=0.3, W=3.0) to follow around the outer edge of the scallops sewing over the cord. This will both strengthen the scalloped edge and give you a more professionally finished edge. You may either use an open toe foot as shown in the top picture or you may use a specialty gimp foot as shown in the lower picture.

Scallops can be plain or fancy. They add an easy elegant finish to napkins, table runners, table cloths and more.

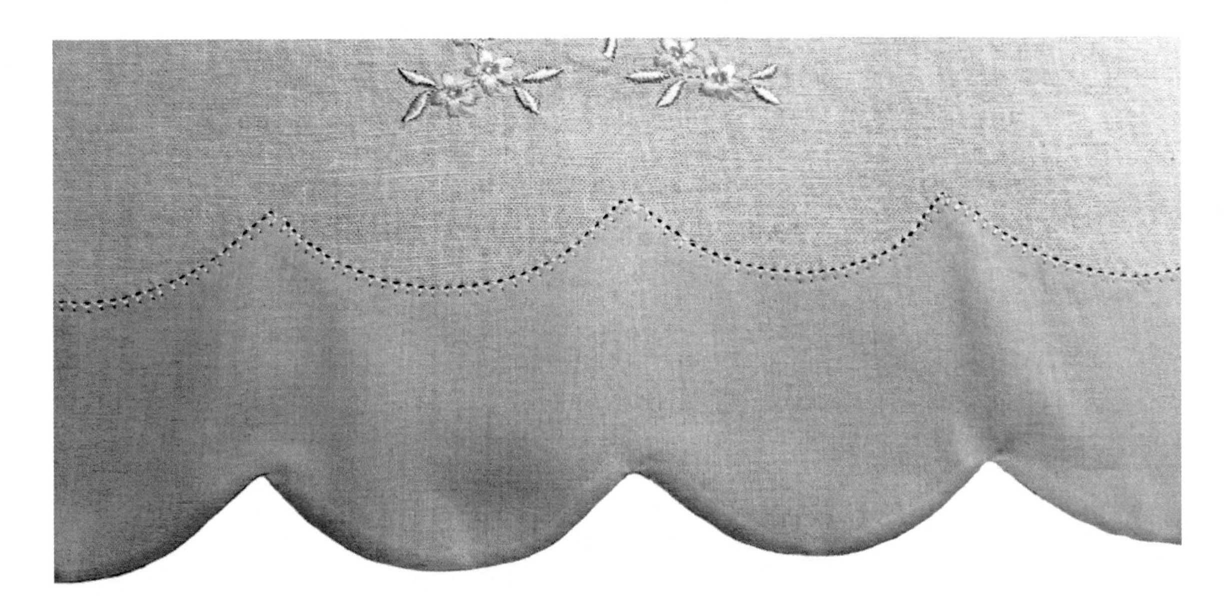

Madeira Appliqué is a method that layers one fabric over another and attaches it using a pin stitch. This technique originated in Madeira, Portugal, and is frequently used for hems. If it is sewn by hand, it is a tedious technique. Sewing it by machine using modern notions is a breeze.

Once this technique is mastered, a Madeira Appliqué adds elegance to any project.

1. Measure a piece of hemming fabric the width of the item by a depth of 4-6 inches and fold it in half. For towels, this will be a long strip; for napkins, table cloths, etc., you will have a large piece folded in half in which you will be sewing around the middle area. See the description of Madeira inserts on page 32 for more information.
2. Using a blue wash-away marker, draw the design from the templates section of this book, or one of your own, onto half of your hemming material.
3. Place wash-away basting thread in the bobbin and lightweight thread in the top of your sewing machine.

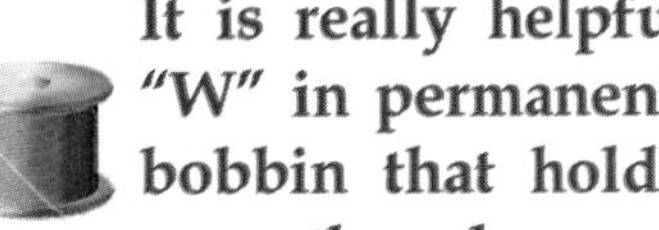

It is really helpful to draw a "W" in permanent ink on the bobbin that holds the wash-away thread.

4. Using a very small stitch (L=1.5) stitch along the marked line (see photo A above).
5. Take the wash-away basting thread out of the bobbin. This step is ***very important***. You do not want to finish your project with wash-away thread – trust me on this one!
6. Trim the inside or top edge of the design to ¼ inch, clipping corners as needed. Do not clip too closely to the edge. You need this as a seam allowance in a later step (see photo B).
7. Turn the design right side out. Use a point turner on the points if needed to keep them sharp.
8. Press the design flat using a dry iron. If you need to clip an area or push the points out further, do so now and re-press it (see photo C).
9. Spray the edge lightly with spray starch. Do not over saturate the fabric with the starch.
10. Press the design until it is ***completely*** dry.
11. Repeat steps 9 and 10 twice more.
12. Gently pull the design open (see photo D). If it doesn't pull apart easily, repeat steps 9 and 10 again.
13. Lay the item to be hemmed on your work surface wrong side up.

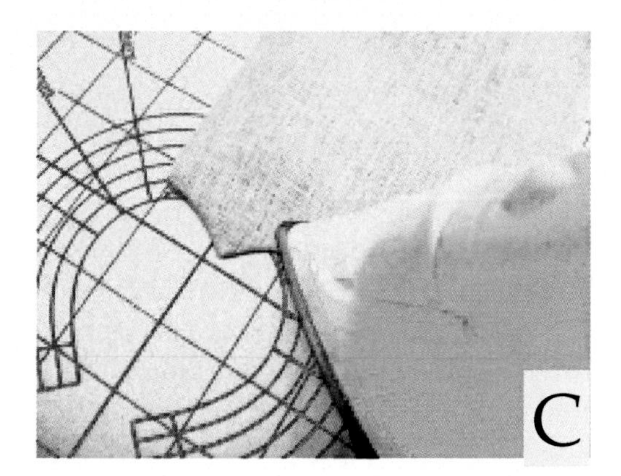

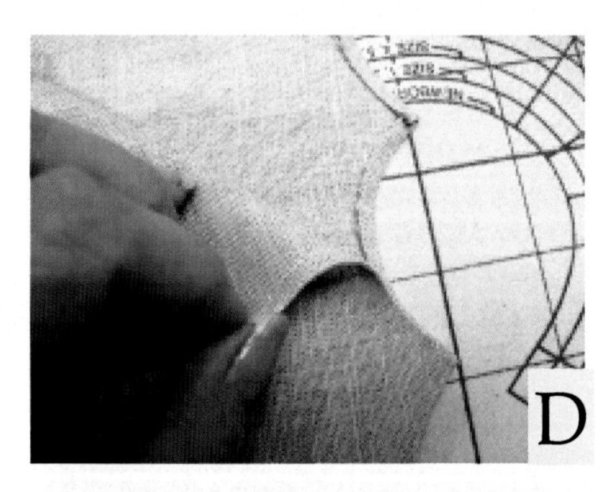

14. Lay the design onto your item wrong side up and pin the bottom of the pieces together. *Yes, this is both pieces wrong side up.* This is very important.
15. Stitch the hem. The hem may be straight or curved.
16. Turn and press the piece. You will now have right sides up.
17. Use a temporary spray adhesive to hold the appliqué in place.
18. Place strips of wash-away stabilizer under the area to be stitched.
19. Stitch down the hem top using a pin stitch with the "teeth" biting into the appliqué design and the straight part of the stitch running along the edge of the design. Alternatively you can use a small zigzag to hold down the appliqué and follow up with a reinforced straight stitch along the edge of the design (see photo E on previous page).
20. Tear away the stabilizer and press.

Madeira appliqué takes many forms, scallops (top), inserts (above) or straight edges (right).

Madeira Appliqué is not only a hemming technique, it may also be used to create beautiful inserts. Madeira inserts are generally made from a different fabric than the main fabric.

1. Fold your fabric in half and using a blue wash-away marker, draw the design from the templates section of this book (or one of your own) onto half of your material.
2. Place wash-away basting thread in the bobbin and lightweight thread in the top of your sewing machine.
3. Using a very small stitch (L=1.5) stitch along the marked line (see photo A on page 30).
4. Take the wash-away basting thread out of the bobbin. This step is ***very important***. You do not want to finish your project with wash-away thread.
5. Trim the inside edge of the design to ¼ inch, clipping corners as needed. Do not clip too closely to the edge. You need this as a seam allowance in a later step (see photo B on page 30).
6. Turn the design right side out. Use a point turner on the points if needed to keep them sharp.
7. Press the design flat using a dry iron. If you need to clip an area or push the points out further, do so now and re-press it (see photo C on page 30).
8. Spray the edge lightly with spray starch. Do not over saturate with the starch.
9. Press the design until it is ***completely*** dry.
10. Repeat steps 8 and 9 twice more.
11. Gently pull the design open (see photo D page 30). If it doesn't pull apart easily, repeat steps 8 and 9 again.

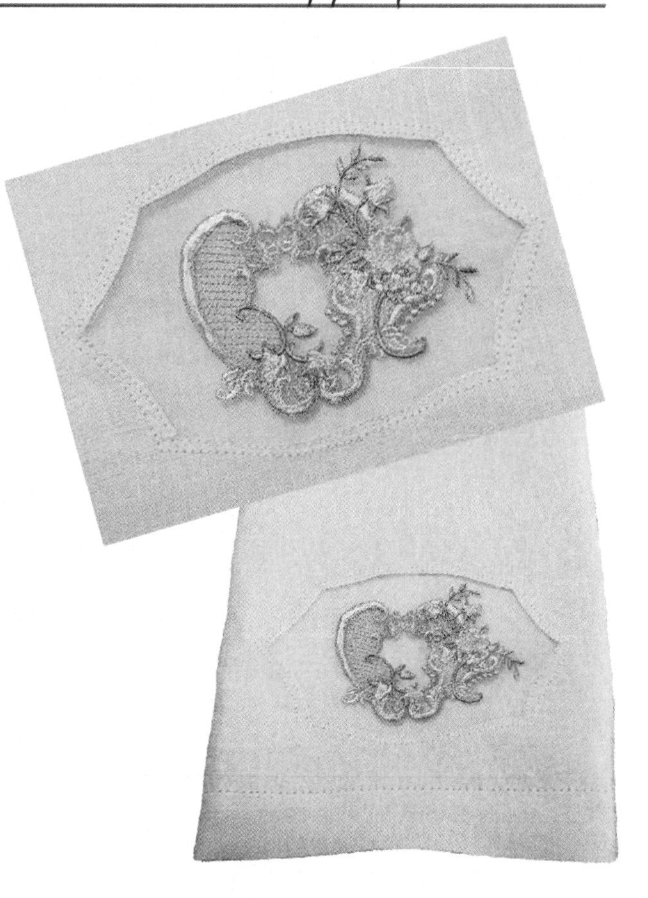

The fabric for the inserts shown above is organdy.

12. Place the design under the insert area you have created.
13. Use a temporary spray adhesive to hold the insert and the fabric in place.
14. Place strips of wash-away stabilizer under the insert area.
15. Stitch down the design using a pin stitch with the "teeth" biting into the appliqué design and the straight part of the stitch running along the edge of the design. Alternatively you can use a small zigzag to hold down the appliqué and a reinforced straight stitch along the edge of the design (see photo E page 30).
16. Tear away the stabilizer and press.

You can add transparency to things you sew using the age-old technique of lace shaping. It is a technique equally at home with home decor as it is with christening gowns and women's clothing.

Start with simple shapes. In no time you will be able to shape more complex designs. The shape used for the Windsor Placemats project looks complicated, but it is only slightly more complicated than shaping a diamond or heart.

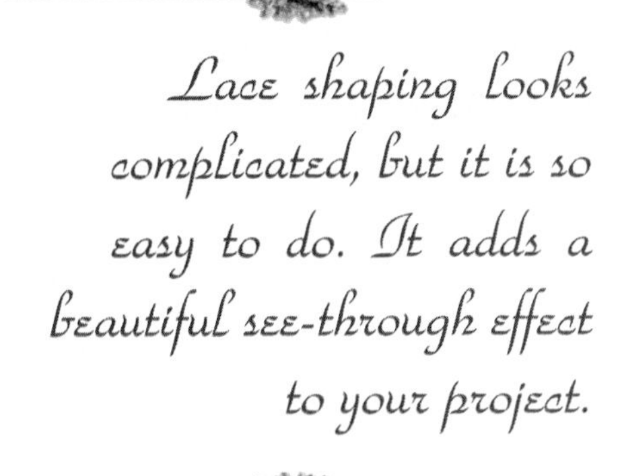

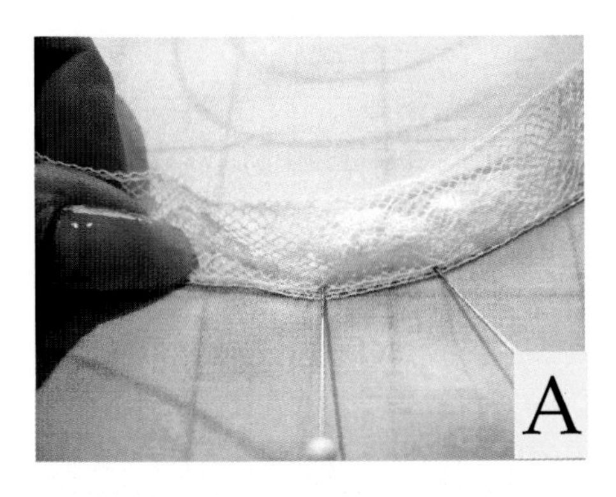

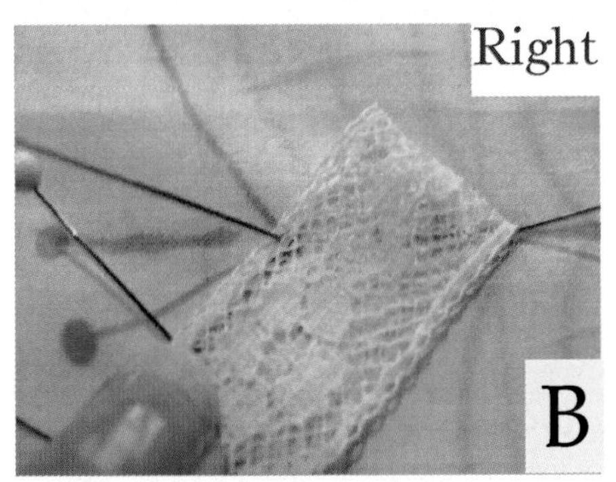

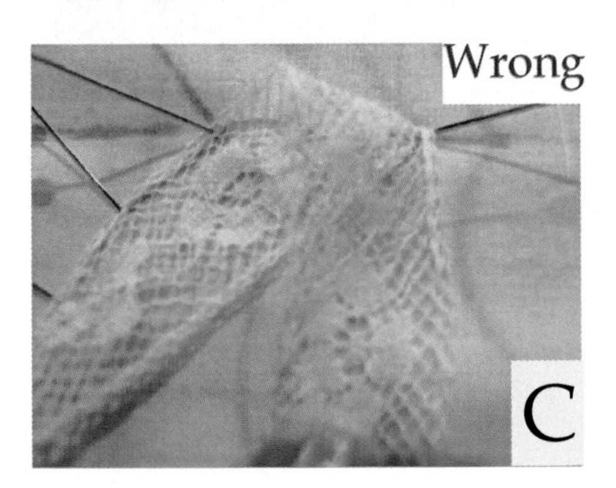

1. Draw the template from the CD in this book (or one of your own design) onto your fabric using wash-away marker.
2. Pin all four corners of the fabric to a lace shaping board or cloth-covered piece of corrugated cardboard box.
3. Shape the lace around the outside row of the markings using *glass head* pins. Use as many as needed to follow the shape (see photo A). If the shape is a diamond or square, just add a few pins to keep the edges straight.
4. At the corners, pin the inside and outside of the lace (instead of just the outside as you have been doing) at the point where the miter line has been drawn.
5. Fold the lace back upon itself so both sides of the lace are parallel (see photo B). It should be on itself as in the photo, not to the side like photo C.
6. Remove the inside pin and re-pin it over both layers of lace, mitering the corner (see photo D next page).
7. Continue pinning the lace around the design.
8. If the shape is curved, you will have the outside pinned and lots of extra lace on the inside. (see photo E next page)

9. Cotton laces have a header thread that you can pull (see photo F).
10. Pull the header thread gently until the inside of the lace lays flat (see photo G). It is usually best to pull one side of the lace shape and then pull the header lace around the other side rather than pulling all the way around.
11. Take the piece to the ironing board and *lightly* spray starch it.
12. Press it completely dry.
13. Lightly spray starch it again and press it dry again so your lace piece is quite stiff.
14. Carefully remove the piece from the board. At this point, you only need to replace a few of the pins; just enough to keep the lace in place as you sew.
15. Using a small zigzag (L=2.0, W=2.0), zigzag around one or both sides of the lace, depending upon the project directions, making sure the stitches go over the lace header.
16. Carefully cut a center line behind the lace creating a 1/4 inch seam allowance, being careful not to cut the lace (see photo H on page 35).
17. Where the lace shape is curved, clip this seam allowance where necessary and press the seam allowance ***away*** from the lace (see page 35 H and I).

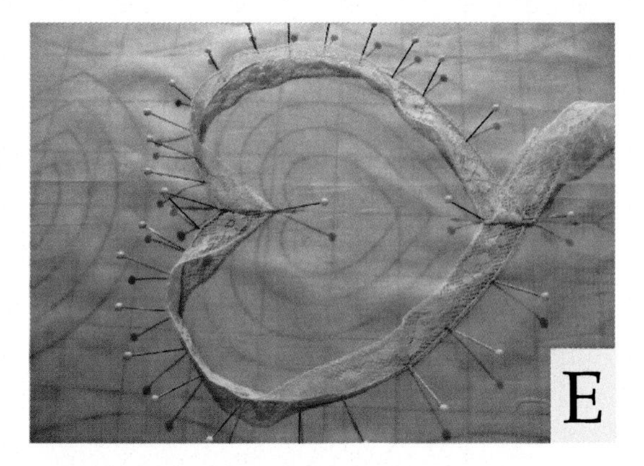
E

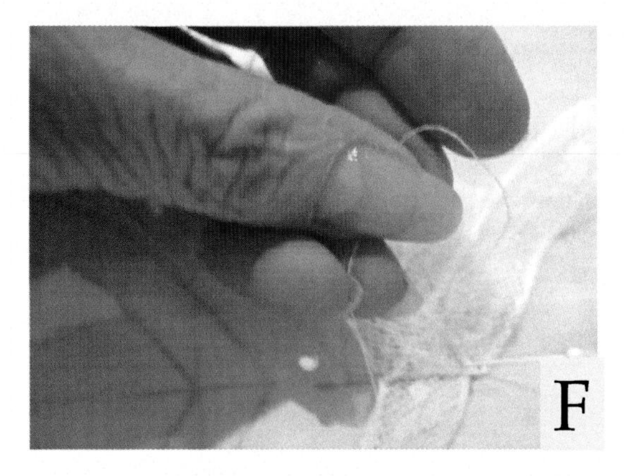
F

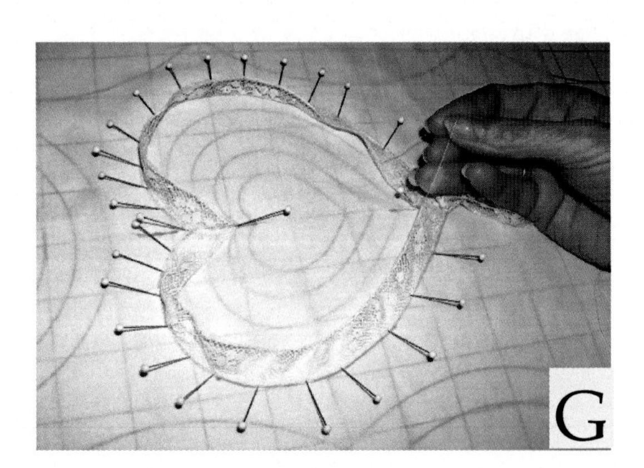
G

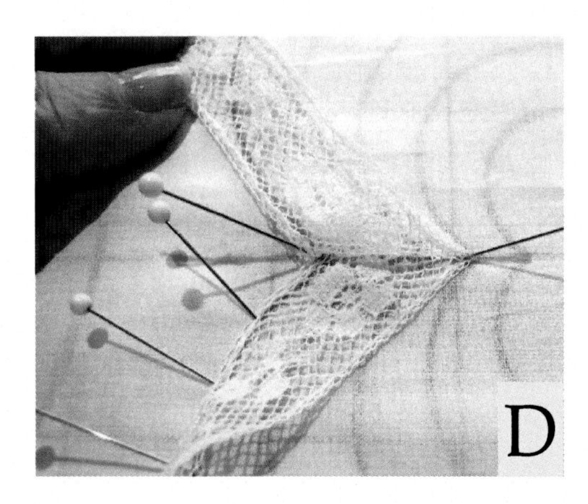
D

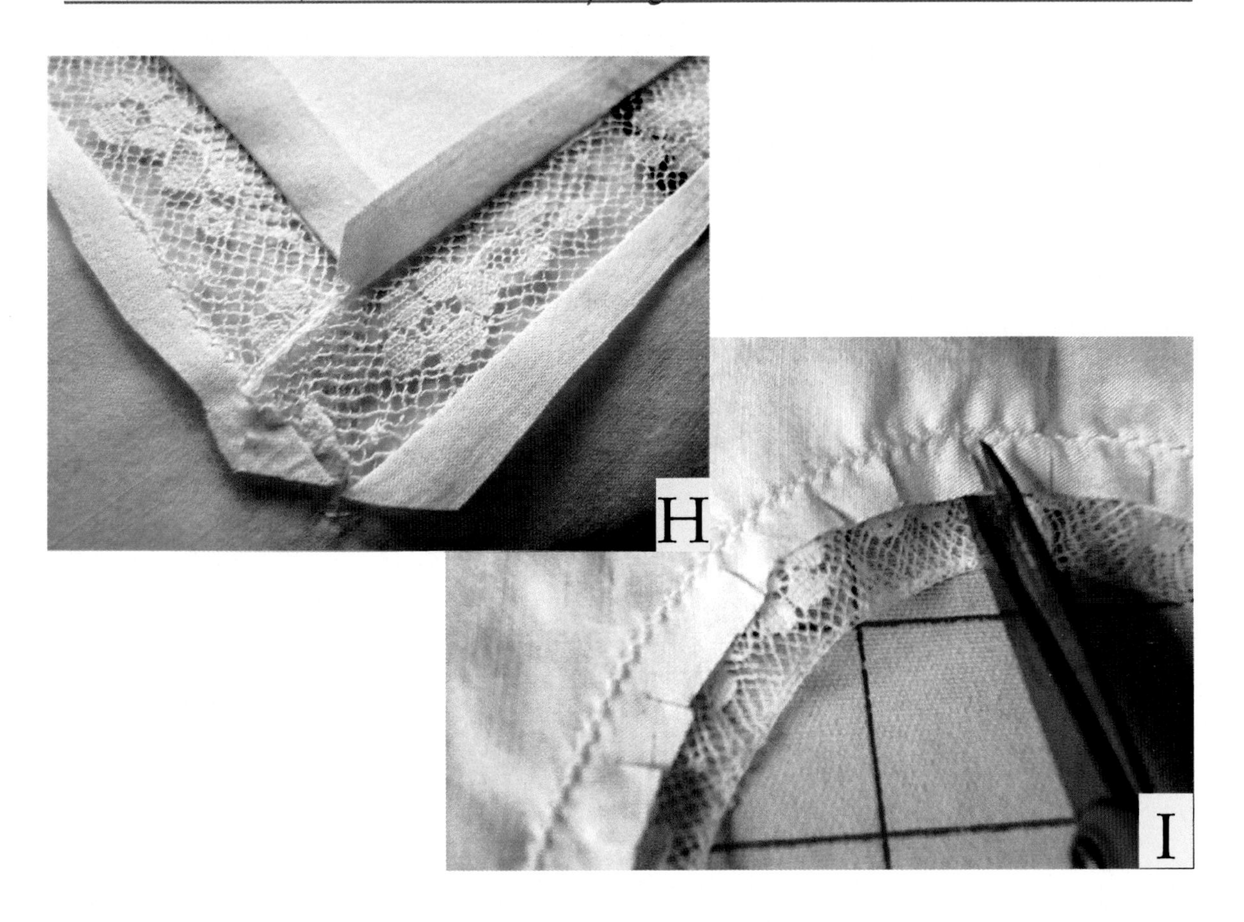

18. Zigzag (L=1.5, W=1.5) along all miter fold lines.
19. Remove the extra lace in the miter cutting as close to the stitches as possible without cutting the zigzag stitches.
20. Using a wing needle and paper stabilizer, entredeux or pin stitch (L=2.5, W=3.0) sew around one or both sides of the lace according to the project directions.
21. Trim away the excess seam allowance from behind the lace (see photo J).
22. Follow the instructions from the individual project you are working on for sewing the lace to the item.

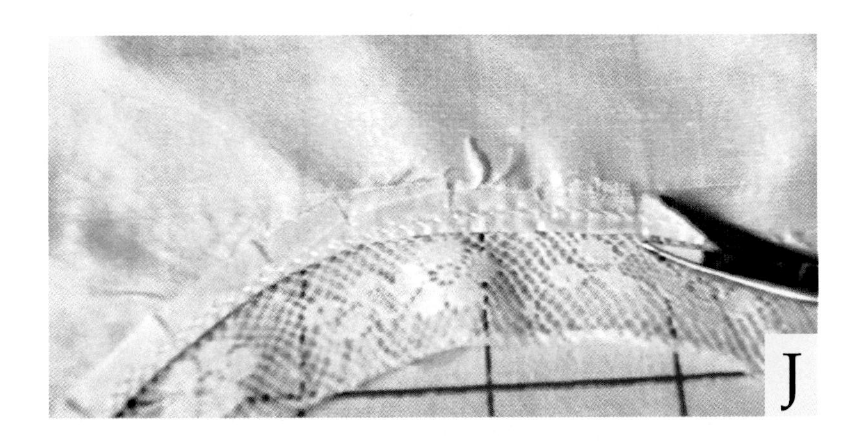

Once you try adding gimp work to your projects, you'll be hooked. It adds a delicate raised texture that frames other design elements in your work.

Gimp work is a technique where you cover a fine cord with a satin stitch or tight zigzag stitch. Years ago it was done completely by hand and took months to complete.

Gimp work adds beautiful finishing touch to your work. This raised technique can be added just about anywhere. You can sew gimp work along a hemline or surround a shaped lace area with it. Draw squiggly lines with a blue marker and run the gimp work along it. Use it any way you want. If you have a special gimp foot for your sewing machine, it makes this technique a breeze to do.

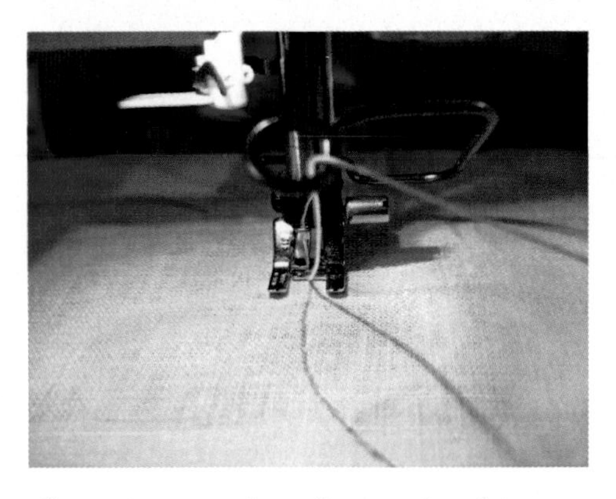

If you have a gimp foot and guide, you only need to "drive the fabric" along the line as shown above.

If you don't have a gimp foot, use an open toe foot and lay the gimp along the line as you sew.

To stitch the gimp cord down to your fabric, use a narrow satin stitch (L=0.3, W=2.0) or the tightest zigzag stitch you have with a width of 2.0. Proceed as follows:

1. Place tear-away stabilizer under the entire area of the design.
2. Start the gimp work with a 1 to 2 inch gimp cord tail at one side of the gimp line.
3. Continue sewing all around the gimp line you are following.
4. At the curves, stop with the needle down on the outside of the curve, pivot the piece and continue.
5. If you are sewing in a complete circle, stop with the needle down about 2 inches before you get to the point where you started, otherwise, just sew to the end of your line.
6. Pull the gimp cord at the beginning of the stitching until the fabric gathers slightly. Cut the excess gimp cord. Straighten out the gathers. This will cause the excess gimp cord to be drawn inside the stitched area.
7. If you are sewing in a circle, finish the remaining 2 inches then stitch over the beginning stitches (being careful not to stitch on the cord) to overlap about 1/32 inch. Repeat step 6 for the cord end.
8. Remove the stabilizer and press.

The first time I ever saw this technique, I thought to myself, "how can this work?" How can one do such a tight zigzag stitch without it being ridged and distorting the delicate lace? Well, the answer is in the weight of the thread.

1. Place the lace a scant ¼ inch from the edge of the fabric. Do not place it too close or the fabric won't roll when you zigzag (see photos A and B).
2. Using 60-80 weight cotton thread, sew over the seam allowance and the lace header with a very tight zigzag (L=1.0 W=4.0) stitch. This will create a rolled edge (see photo B). The zig should go over the lace header and the zag should go off the edge of the fabric. Increase the stitch width if needed to make sure the zag goes off the edge of the fabric.

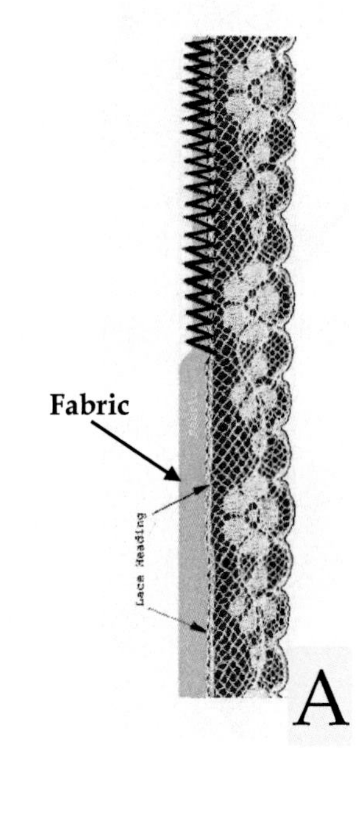

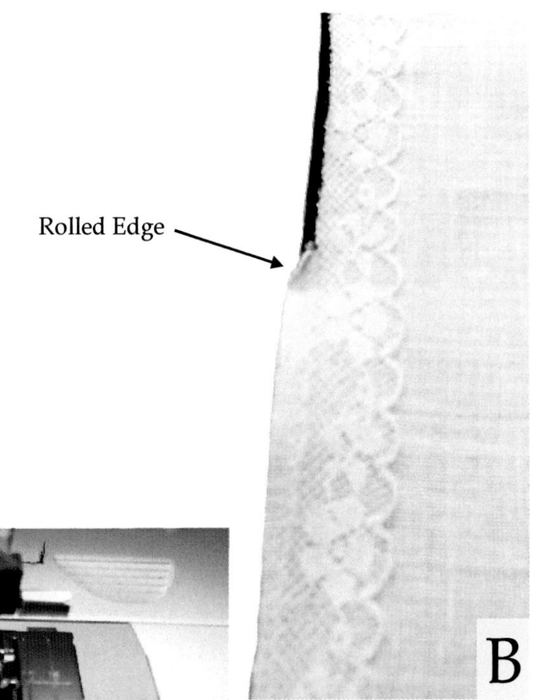

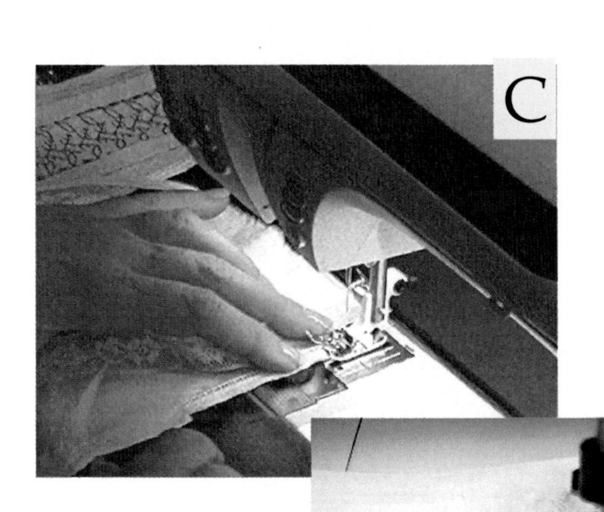

In white, as shown to the above and to the left, you'll have a tiny rolled edge that is almost invisible.

The header of the lace about ¼ inch from edge of fabric. Black thread is used above to show the stitching.

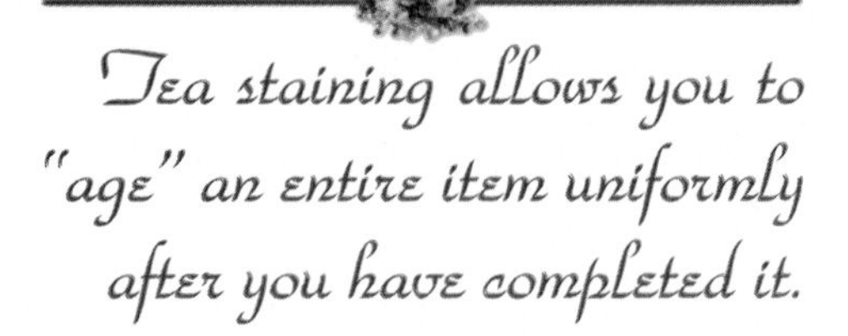

> *Tea staining allows you to "age" an entire item uniformly after you have completed it.*

Tea staining is a one of those ideas that makes us wonder "who thought of that?" They were probably trying to cover up a coffee or tea stain on a table cloth and found it was a great way to add instant age to any home decor item or even a garment. Tea gives a subtle taupe color that is hard to duplicate using dye. If you want a stronger color, use coffee instead of tea. Follow these simple steps to tea stain your project:

1. Use only natural thread, fabric and lace when making your project.
2. If you are embroidering the item, use cotton thread. The whites will turn taupe and the colors will soften.
3. Brew a 2 cup pot of strong tea or coffee. It should be a little stronger than you would normally drink.
4. Empty the pot into a large bowl and add to it about ¼ cup of vinegar.
5. Wet your item in water and carefully wring out the excess.
6. Dunk your item into the bowl. Keep swishing it around so the liquid doesn't settle into the folds.
7. The longer you leave the item in the tea, the darker it will be. However, remember that it will dry about two shades lighter than it looks when wet.
8. Take the item out and rinse it in cool water until the water runs clear.
9. Repeat steps 6 through 8 until the color is pleasing to you.
10. Let the item completely dry on a flat surface. Do not iron it dry or the color will not be even.
11. Heat set the stain by either placing the item in the dryer for about 30 minutes or by ironing it on a medium setting after it is dry.

Now that we've covered the basics, let's get to the fun stuff

. . . the projects!

We'll start with towels: they are a simple way to "test" our skills before we move on to more complex projects. As you work through the projects in this book you'll learn new techniques while making beautiful-romantic home decor for yourself or for giving as gifts.

Towels are a wonderful way to practice techniques. They are quick and inexpensive. You can easily and quickly make beautiful towels for your kitchen, or your friends'.

The following pages also include instructions for turning your towel into a bottle carrier. Give your hostess a gift of wine, juice or even a bottle of bubbly (bubble bath that is) in a bottle carrier made from a towel. Any of the towels in this section may be converted to a bottle carrier with just a couple of basting stitches and a cord so that you have a gift that "keeps on giving" long after the bottle is empty. The instructions for the bottle carrier are given after the general instructions for towels below.

General Supplies for Towels

- 5/8 yard medium weight linen in the color specified in the directions
- 60 weight cotton sewing thread to match the linen color
- 40 weight embroidery thread in the colors specified in the directions
- Size 80 machine embroidery needle
- Size 75 universal machine needle
- Size 120 wing needle
- Double stick fusible tape (if hemstitching)
- Wash-away marker
- Stabilizer as called for in the directions

Nothing feels quite like a soft 100 percent linen towel whether lining a tea tray, drying fine crystal, or drying everyday dishes. Reaching in your drawer and pulling out a beautiful towel to dry your dishes takes some of the drudgery out of washing up.

General Directions for Towels

1. Pull threads in the linen (see the Basics section page 15) to create a rectangle that is 20 inches (width) by 33 inches (length) for hemstitched towels, 20 by 39 inches for Madeira edged towels and 20 by 30½ inches for all other towels.
2. If you do not have a serger, skip to step 6.
3. If your serger has a cover stitch, use it to serge down both sides of the towel.
4. Finish the back and if instructed to, the front of the towel with a 4 thread overlock. Go to step 9.
5. If you have a serger that does not have a cover stitch, use a four thread overlock along each of the lengthwise sides. Skip to step 7.
6. If you do not have a serger, use your sewing machine's overcast stitch or zigzag to finish the lengthwise sides.
7. Fold over the two side edges (the 30½ or 32 inch sides) to the wrong side about ¼ inch and press.
8. Sew the pressed edges down with a straight stitch.
9. Fold the back edge to the wrong side creating a ½ inch hem.
10. Sew the hem with either a straight stitch or an entredeux stitch using the wing needle.
11. Hem the front of the towel using stabilizer as instructed in the individual instructions.
12. Measure and mark the placement for the embroidery centered from side to side and up from the edge as stated in the individual instructions.
13. Embroider the design centered on the placement mark.
14. Follow any remaining instructions in the individual design.

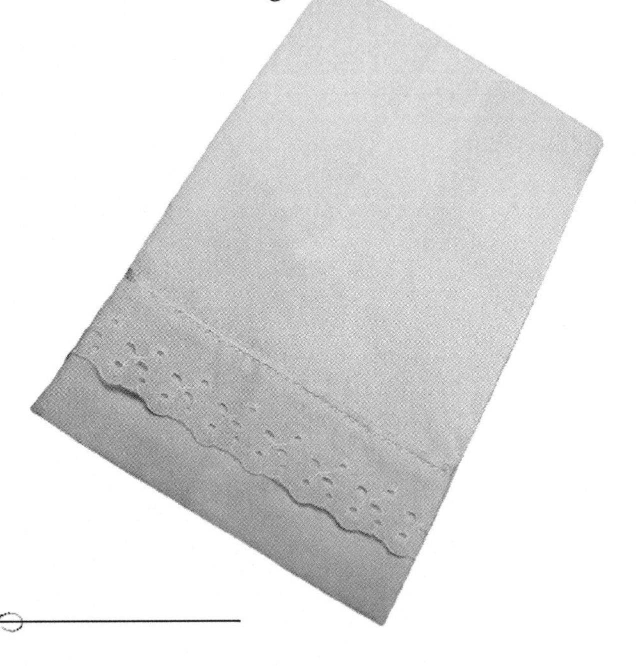

Take this thoughtful gift to a friend. They will appreciate it for many years, not just one night. If you don't want to take wine, try a "bit of bubbly"–.bubble bath, that is.

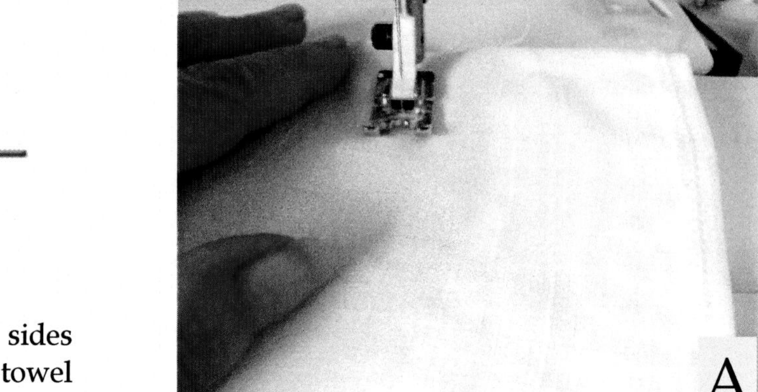

Basting the side seams

1. Fold the towel crosswise, right sides together, with the front (where the towel design is) extending two to three inches above the back to create a flap (see diagram below).
2. Baste each side of the towel (L=5.0) creating a 3 inch seam on each side of the towel (see photo A).
3. Match the basted seam to the bottom fold creating a point. Sew across the towel, creating a flat bottom (see photo B).
4. Turn the towel right side out.
5. Side the bottle into the opening.
6. Place a grommet or punch a hole into the tag.
7. Measure a 24 inch cord and slide the tag onto it. Tie the cord in a bow around the bottle neck and towel.
8. Fold the front flap over the cord so the design shows.

Sewing the towel point, creating a flat bottom for the holder.

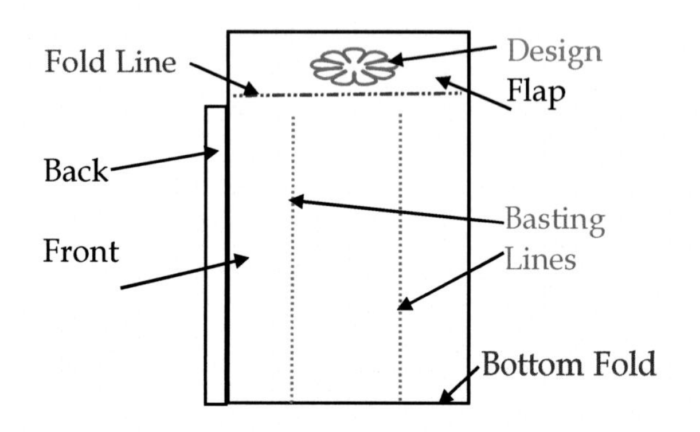

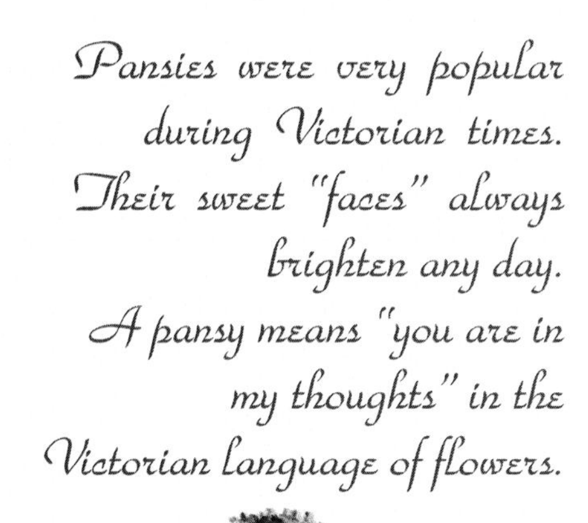

Make this towel in the muted colors as shown, or match your own kitchen colors. Pansies come in every color in the rainbow and even black and orange. So only the sky is the limit to your creativity.

Supplies

- Supplies from the basic towel supplies on page 41
- Pansy embroidery design from the CD in this book
- 40 weight Rayon embroidery thread in the following Sulky® colors:
  1. 1165 soft blue
  2. 1211 muted green
  3. 1213 muted mauve
  4. 1179 dark taupe

Directions

1. Follow the general instructions, finishing the sides, front and back of the towel on page 41.
2. The embroidered design will be centered from side to side and approximately 7 inches from the front bottom of the towel. As an option, embroider a name or a saying below the design.
3. Follow the instructions for hemstitching on page 21.

Delicate machine embroidery pairs up with a Madeira Appliqué hem to make this stunning towel. Sure to be a favorite.

This towel is embroidered in muted shades to give it an antique look. The linen Madeira appliqué hem is in a muted taupe that matches the outline stitches in the design.

Supplies

- Basic towel supplies from page 41
- Taupe linen 6 inches by 22 inches for the Madeira appliqué
- Floral design from the CD in this book
- 40 weight Rayon embroidery thread in the following Sulky® colors:
  1. 1321 Muted-dusty green
  2. 1297 Muted purple
  3. 1304 Mauve
  4. 1213 Light mauve
  5. 1070 Light gold
  6. 1127 Dark ecru
  7. 1291 Dusty blue
  8. 1549 Flax

Note: You may wish to choose other colors to match your décor and to use cotton fabric instead of linen for the appliqué.

Directions

1. Follow the general instructions, finishing 3 sides of the towel from page 41. The bottom edge of the embroidery should be at least 4½ inches from the bottom edge of the towel front.
2. Follow the instructions for Madeira hemming on page 29.

A bit of exquisite lace and a muted rose monogram turns an otherwise plain towel into something special.

These towels are perfect for laying on a tea tray or for drying crystal. This design is particularly suited for a bottle carrier because the lace adds extra length to the towel.

Supplies

- Basic towel supplies from page 41
- ½ yard 4 inch Rayon lace with a straight edge
- Temporary spray adhesive
- Embroidery Monogram from the CD in this book
- 40 weight Rayon embroidery thread in the following Sulky® colors:
  1. 1549 Flax
  2. 1321 Muted-dusty green
  3. 1297 Muted purple
  4. 1304 Mauve

Directions

1. Cut the towel - Prepare the towel as described in the general towel directions on page 41, finishing 3 sides of the towel.
2. Embroider the design centered from side to side and approximately 3-4 inches from the front cut edge of the towel.
3. Follow the instructions for a lace hem, method two on page 26.

Now that you have mastered towels, it's time to try napkins, placemats table runners and table cloths. These have 4 finished sides, making them a little more challenging than towels, but don't worry, you're ready.

Placemat with drawn thread hemstitching, gimp work, decorative stitching and monogram.

Long ago, napkins were monogrammed or embellished in order for the owner to know that the napkin belonged to them when it came time for dinner. In earlier days, table linens were not washed after each use as they are today. Each person needed to know which napkin was theirs to help prevent the spread of germs and to be at least a *little* more hygienic. Thank goodness, we now can have the beauty of an embellished napkin and wash them too!

Add elegance to your tables with linen napkins, placemats and table runners. Make everyday meals seem special.

The napkins in our projects are made of linen. Not only does linen hold up to repeated washings, it also has such a wonderful hand. If you prefer, your napkins can be made of cotton or blends.

Placemats, while less formal than a table cloth, can still be elegant. There are limitless ways to embellish placemats. Any technique used for napkins may be used for placemats. One exception is that you can only add embellishment to the center of a placemat.

Table runners can be used as a decorative element in your room or they can be placed across a table to create place settings (see the Sophisticated Table Runner project on page 58). Like placemats, you can add embellishment to the center, but because they are longer than a placemat, you can also embellish the ends.

General Supplies for Napkins and Table Covers

- Linen Yardage—Medium to Heavyweight
  - ✂ 5/8 yard linen in the weight from the instructions (for 2 napkins) or
  - ✂ ½ yard heavyweight linen (for 2 placemats) or
  - ✂ ½ yard light to medium weight linen (for 1 table runner)
  - ✂ Yardage for table cloths according to the guidelines on page 60
- 60 weight cotton sewing thread to match the napkins
- 40 weight embroidery thread in the colors shown for the specific napkin
- Double stick fusible tape (for hemstitching only)
- Size 80 machine embroidery needle
- Size 80 universal machine needle
- Size 120 wing needle (for hemstitching)
- Size 100 topstitching needle (for pin stitching)
- Double-stick fusible tape (optional)
- Blue wash-away marker
- Stabilizer as called for in the directions

General Directions for Napkins and Table Covers

1. Cut the fabric according to the individual project instructions.
2. Finish all 4 sides according to the project directions, using the finishing instructions in the hemming section from the Basic Techniques section of this book.
3. If you are using a hemstitched edge, follow the instructions for the perfect mitered corner on page 19.

Formal napkins go with everything. Even a simple picnic is better when you have linen napkins.

A book on elegant and romantic kitchen and dining room ideas would not be complete without a napkin for a formal table setting. These simple white linen napkins are as luxurious as they come.

Supplies

- General supplies for napkins on page 47
- 40 weight white embroidery thread
- Wash-away marker
- Monogram of your choice

Directions

1. Cut the linen into a 25 inch square.
2. Follow the general instructions on page 21 for finishing with hemstitching on all four sides. However, instead of pulling 3 threads, pull 4 along each side to make the holes extra large.
3. On one corner, measure 3 inches from the bottom and draw a line with the wash-away marker.
4. Measure 3 inches up from the side edge and draw another line.
5. Place the embroidered design in the corner of the napkin centered where the two lines intersect, keeping the monogram parallel to the side and bottom edge.

These napkins will look as if they have been in your family for years. Sewn in soft yellow linen with a white monogram and white lace they will show off your dishes with style. Since these are casual napkins, the monogram is placed on the diagonal.

Supplies

- General supplies for napkins on page 47 (yellow linen)
- 2 ¾ yards 1 inch white edging lace
- Wash-away marker
- Monogram of your choice from the CD in this book (entire design will be stitched in white thread)
- 40 weight white Rayon thread
- 60 weight cotton thread to match the linen

Directions

1. Cut the linen into a 20½ inch square.
2. Follow the general instructions for finishing a lace edge on all four sides of the napkin.
3. On one corner, measure 4 inches from one side and draw a line with the wash-away marker. Measure 4 inches up from the other edge and draw another line.
4. Place the embroidered design in the corner of the napkin centered where the two lines intersect.

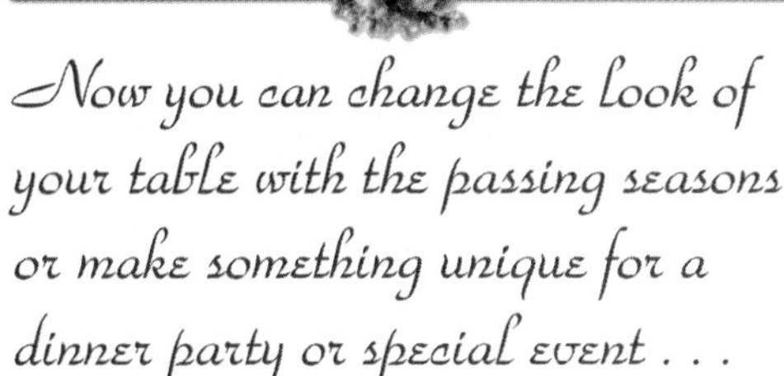

A simple way to change your table with the seasons is to create these napkins. Our designs come with, and without, the season names for you to use—or better yet, embroider the name of the person who will be seated at the table. At your next dinner party, why not sew these napkins for each guest and give them as a party favor? If you host holiday dinners, have a holiday-specific napkin for each member of the family to use year after year.

Supplies

- General supplies for napkins on page 47
- Wash-away marker
- Holiday Embroidery design from the CD or one of your choice

Directions

1. Cut the linen to a 23 inch square.
2. Follow the general instructions for finishing with hemstitching on all four sides on page 21.
3. On one corner, measure 4 inches from one side and draw a line with the wash-away marker. Measure 4 inches up from the other edge and draw another line.
4. Place the embroidered design in the corner of the napkin centered on the *diagonal* where the two lines intersect.

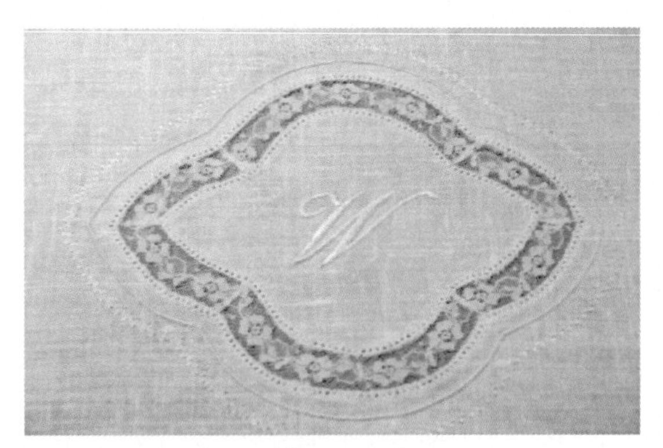

Shaped lace center

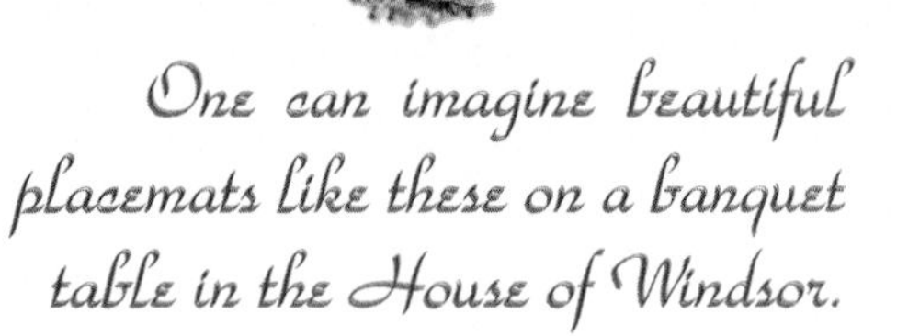

One can imagine beautiful placemats like these on a banquet table in the House of Windsor.

Set an elegant table with these stunning placemats. The mitered hem is embellished with drawn thread work that is secured with wing-needle stitches. Shaped lace is surrounded by gimp work and decorative stitches to accent the center monogram. The gimp work creates a beautiful border for the lace. These techniques are beautifully blended in this impressive placemat—beautiful enough to have been used in the House of Windsor.

Supplies

- General supplies for placemats on page 47
- 3/4 yard 5/8 inch insertion lace
- 2 yards of gimp cording
- #120 wing needle
- 40 weight Rayon embroidery thread - ecru
- 60 weight cotton sewing thread - white and ecru
- Wash-away marker
- Tear-away stabilizer
- Template for lace shaping from page 70
- Open toe foot or gimp foot and guide (optional)

Directions

1. Cut a rectangle of white linen 15½ x 19½ inches for each placemat following the general instructions on page 15 for keeping straight on the grain.
2. Follow the general instructions for hemstitching. Note: the hem should be 1½ inches from the folded edge all the way around creating a 14 x 18 inch mat.
3. Fold the mat in half lengthwise and mark this line with a blue wash-away marker.

4. Fold the mat in half crosswise and mark this line in the same manner.
5. Where the two lines intersect will be your center point for your monogram.
6. Draw the lace shaping template from page 70 around the monogram.
7. Shape your lace around the template line following the general instructions for lace shaping on page 33—sewing around both sides of the lace.
8. Change to your gimping foot, or open toe foot, and engage your machine's "needle down" option if you have it and follow the general directions for gimp work. Stitch the gimp work one presser foot away from the lace.
9. Sew a decorative stitch of your choice around the gimp, one presser foot away from the gimp line.
10. Remove the stabilizer and press.

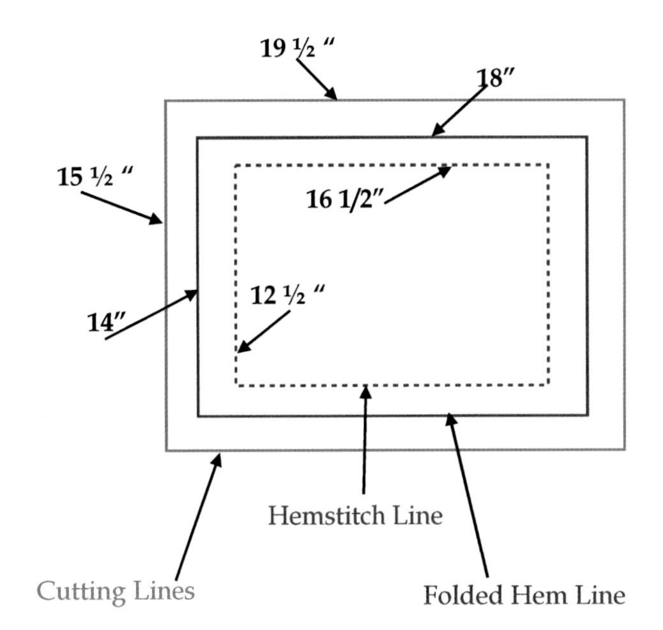

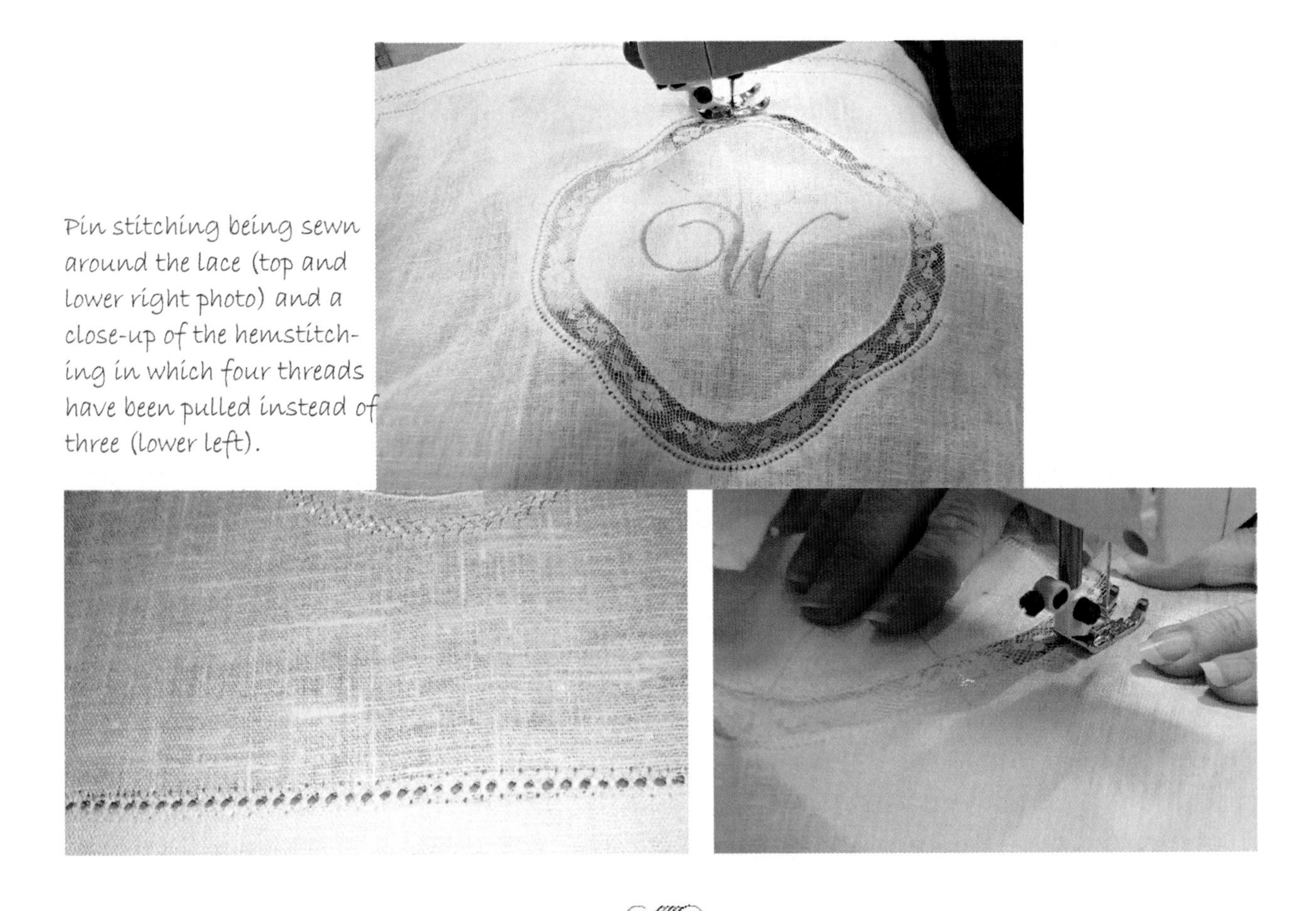

Pin stitching being sewn around the lace (top and lower right photo) and a close-up of the hemstitching in which four threads have been pulled instead of three (lower left).

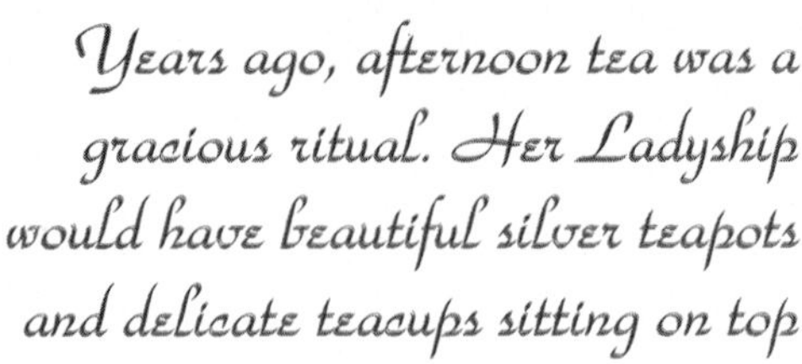

Years ago, afternoon tea was a gracious ritual. Her Ladyship would have beautiful silver teapots and delicate teacups sitting on top of a table cover like this.

Elegant enough to be used in the finest setting, this linen table runner uses beautiful techniques that are a lot of fun to stitch. The center and ends are embellished with pre-made embroidery appliqués. Gimp work accents the lace and creates a beautiful border along the mitered hem that is secured with wing-needle hemstitching. Decorative stitching surrounds the gimp work. These techniques are beautifully blended in this impressive centerpiece.

Supplies

- General supplies for runners on page 47
- 1/3 yard lightweight handkerchief linen for inserts
- 10 yards of gimp cording
- 4 ecru cotton Venetian lace appliqués
- Ecru lightweight sewing thread
- Tear-away stabilizer
- Template for Madeira appliqué from the CD
- Open toe foot or gimp foot and guide (optional)

Cutting

- ✂ Cut a rectangle of white linen 47 x 21 inches for the table runner
- ✂ Cut one piece of the handkerchief linen 10 x 10 inches for the center
- ✂ Cut two pieces of handkerchief linen 6 x 10 inches for the sides

Directions

1. Follow the diagram on page 56 to draw the following lines with a wash-away blue marker on the *wrong* side of the rectangle:
   a. Fold the rectangle in half lengthwise and draw a line to mark the vertical fold.
   b. Fold the rectangle in half crosswise and draw a line to mark the horizontal fold.
   c. Measure 7 inches down from each side of the horizontal center line on the rectangle and draw a line. This will be the fold line for the hem on each side of the table runner.

d. Measure 20 inches each down from each side of the vertical center line on the rectangle and draw a line. This will be the fold line for the hem on each end of the table runner.
e. Mark 2 inches above the end fold lines (18 inches from the original center line) for the placement of the Madeira appliqué on each end. The bottom stitching line will be placed on this line.

2. Iron the hems along the drawn hemlines pressing the hem toward the wrong side of the fabric.
3. With *right* sides together folded on the crosswise line, draw the half of the Madeira template in the center of the table runner, matching the lengthwise center line.
4. With *right* sides together, folded on the lengthwise line, trace the end template on each end of the runner. Make sure the bottom straight stitching line is on the line marked in step 1e and the fold line is on the lengthwise fold line.

Table runner center

Table runner end.

Sewing along the blue lines

5. Place one of the appliqués in the center of each of the 6 x 10 inch linen pieces and secure in place with temporary spray adhesive.
6. Place two appliques in the center of the 10x10 inch piece of linen (use the picture below as a guide).
7. Stitch around the appliqués using a small zigzag stitch (L= 1.5, W=1.5).
8. Draw the inserts area onto the main linen piece using the templates on pages 71-72.
9. Follow the directions on page 32 to create the center and end Madeira appliqué openings on the main piece.
10. Pin the 6 x 10 inch piece in the middle of the opening at each end of the table runner. The points of the appliqués should face the center of the runner.

Don't make yourself crazy. Follow the blue lines the best you can. No one will see them once they are washed away.

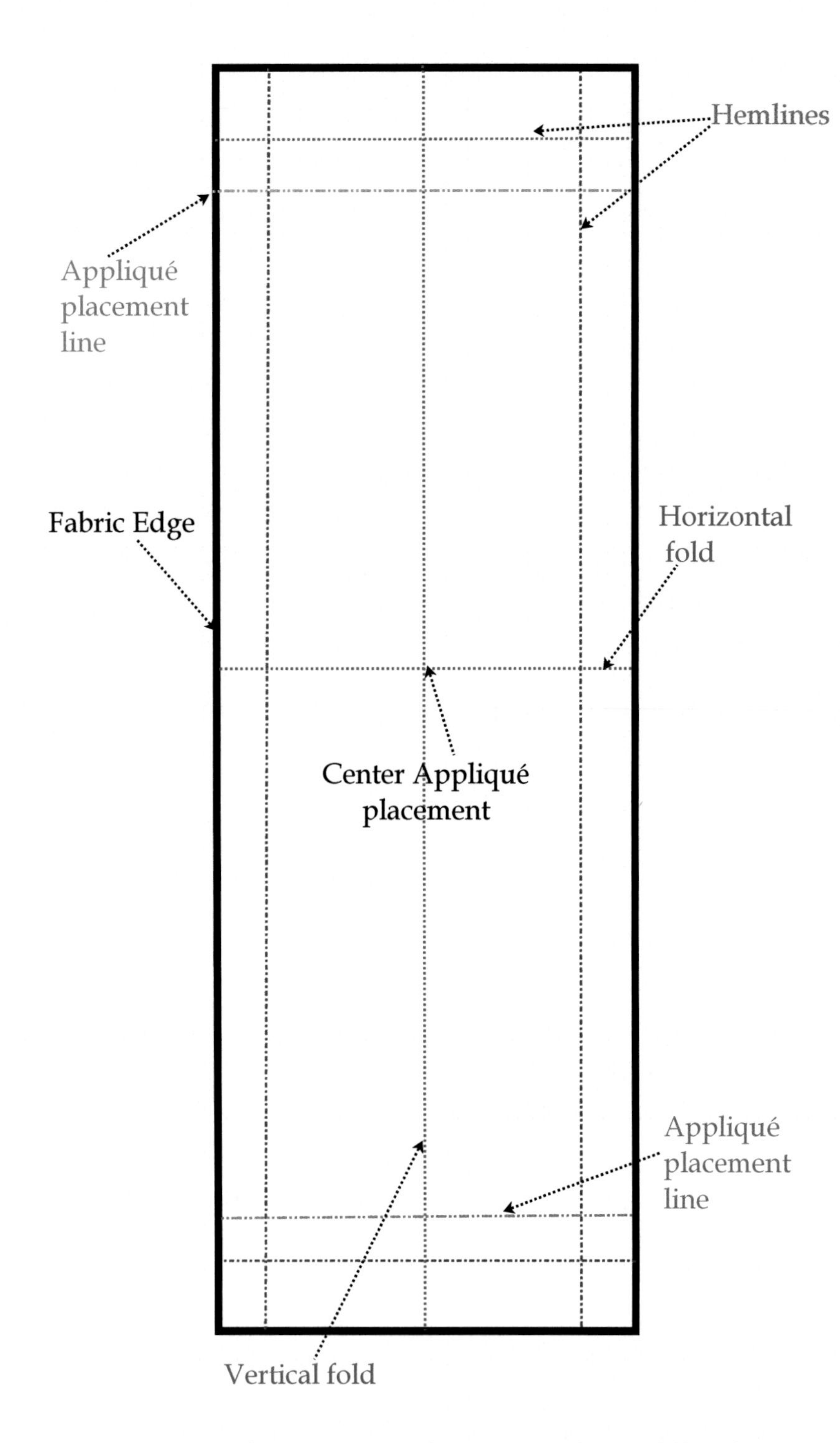

11. Pin the 10 x 10 inch piece in the middle of the opening in the center of the table runner. The points of the appliqués should face the ends of the runner.
12. Sew the appliqué pieces to the runner using a small zigzag (L=1.5, W=1.5).
13. Pin stitch (L=4.0, W=3.0) with a #120 wing needle around the opening. The straight part of the pin stitch should go along the edge inside on the handkerchief linen; the "teeth" of the pin stitch should completely catch the runner linen.
14. Remove the stabilizer. Trim away the handkerchief linen backing as close as possible to outer pin stitch row.
15. Following the general instructions miter the corners of the piece. Note: the raw edges will not match up. Line up the hemlines for your 45 degree stitch line.
16. Using an entredeux stitch (L=4.0, W=3.5), stitch 1½ inches away from the hemline fold into the fabric around all four sides.
17. Trim away the excess fabric from the hem as close to the entredeux stitches as you can without cutting the stitches.
18. Using your gimping foot or open toe foot, and engaging your needle down, stitch the gimp cord down along the edge of the center Madeira appliqué. Use the presser foot as a guide and follow the general gimp work directions on page 36.
19. Stitch a row of gimp work above the hemstitching line using your presser foot as a guide and following around the Madeira appliqué on each edge. (Use the pictures on page 54-55 as a guide).
20. Using a feather stitch (L=2.0, W=4.5) or a decorative stitch of your choice, stitch around the gimp work using your presser foot as a guide.

This runner will add romance to any table. Despite how it looks, it is simple to make and can easily be made on any sewing machine. The Irish linen is dripping with Venetian lace. The finished result looks like it took hours, but it really is quick and easy to make.

A table runner such as this, dripping with lace, will add instant romance to any room.

Supplies

- ½ yard handkerchief weight Irish linen
- 1 yard of 3½ inch Venetian lace with a scalloped edge
- 8 inch square of tear-away stabilizer
- 40 weight Rayon embroidery thread
- 60 weight cotton sewing thread
- 75 machine sewing needle
- Blunt end scissors
- Wash-away blue marker

Instructions

1. Cut the linen to 16½ x 28 inches.
2. If you have a serger, overlock the long edges. If not, zigzag over the edges.
3. Turn under the 28 inch edges to make a ¼ inch hem and stitch with a straight stitch.
4. Alternatively, if you have a serger with a cover stitch, press under the long edges ¼ inch and cover stitch over the raw edges.
5. Pin the lace along the 16 inch edge.
6. Using a small zigzag (L=2.0, W=2.0) zigzag along the top edge of the lace making sure to keep the design straight.
7. Zigzag again about 1/8 inch away from the first stitching. Do not stitch too far away from the first row of stitching.
8. Using the blunt-end scissors, cut away the extra fabric from behind the lace as close to the last row of zigzag without cutting the stitches.
9. With the extra lace, cut two designs to form two medallions for the center of the piece.
10. Fold the piece into quarters to find the center.
11. Place the medallions 3½ inches from the crosswise center line and along the lengthwise center line so they are 7 inches appart.
12. Using a small zigzag (L=2.0, W=2.0) zigzag around the medallion making sure to keep the design straight.
13. Zigzag again about 1/8 inch away from the first stitching.
14. Using the blunt-end scissors, cut away the extra fabric from behind the lace.
15. With a blue wash-away marker, draw 2 curved lines connecting the medallions.
16. Choose a decorative stitch or use gimp work and sew on the blue lines you marked in step 15.
17. Wash out the marker and iron the piece.
18. Lay on table, stand back and admire your beautiful work.

Decorative Stitching connecting the medallions

You don't always have to add lace to create an elegant table runner. This one is pared down to allow the luxurious linen to take center stage.

These simple-to-make table runners replace a table cloth and allow your beautiful table to peak through. The runners are placed *across* the table, one runner acting as a placemat for *two* people who are sitting across from one another.

Note: all seam allowances are ½ inch.

Supplies

- 1 1/8 yards white medium weight linen
- ¼ yard taupe medium weight linen
- 3 yards gimp cord
- 2 yards tear-away stabilizer
- 30 weight Rayon thread in taupe and white
- 60 weight white cotton thread

Cutting

✂ Measure the width of your table. Add 5 inches. This is the length of the white linen.

✂ Cut two pieces of linen 21 inches (width) by the length of the white linen from above. Follow the general directions for keeping on grain.

✂ Cut two pieces of taupe linen 21 by 13 inches.

Directions

1. On one piece of the white linen, draw a line with the wash-away marker 16½ inches from each end. Measure 10½ inches from each side and draw a line across the first line. Where the two lines intersect, will be the center of your gimp work.
2. Draw the scroll lines along this horizontal line keeping them 1 inch away from the center.
3. Follow the general directions for gimp work along the scroll lines using taupe thread.
4. Sew one piece of the taupe linen to each end of the piece of white linen to which you just added the gimp.
5. With right sides together, sew the second piece of white linen to each end of the taupe linen. This will create a giant fabric tube.
6. Press the seams flat.

7. Lay the piece flat with right sides together, matching the seams where the white and taupe connect.
8. Sew down one side completely.
9. Sew down the other side, leaving a 6 inch gap in the white linen for turning.
10. Turn the piece right side out. Make sure the corners are pushed out to a crisp point.
11. Press the piece well.
12. With the *white thread,* topstitch the *taupe* linen 1/8 inch away from the seam line where the taupe and white come together.
13. With the *taupe* thread, topstitch the *white* linen 1/8 inch away from the seam line where the taupe and white come together.

Imagine you could hold the sewn linen pieces and look at them edge on, they would look like a circular tube as shown below. The wrong side of the fabric is outside and the right side of the fabric is on the inside. This "tube" is then flattened out with right sides together, matching the seam lines where the taupe and white linen join, and then sew as described.

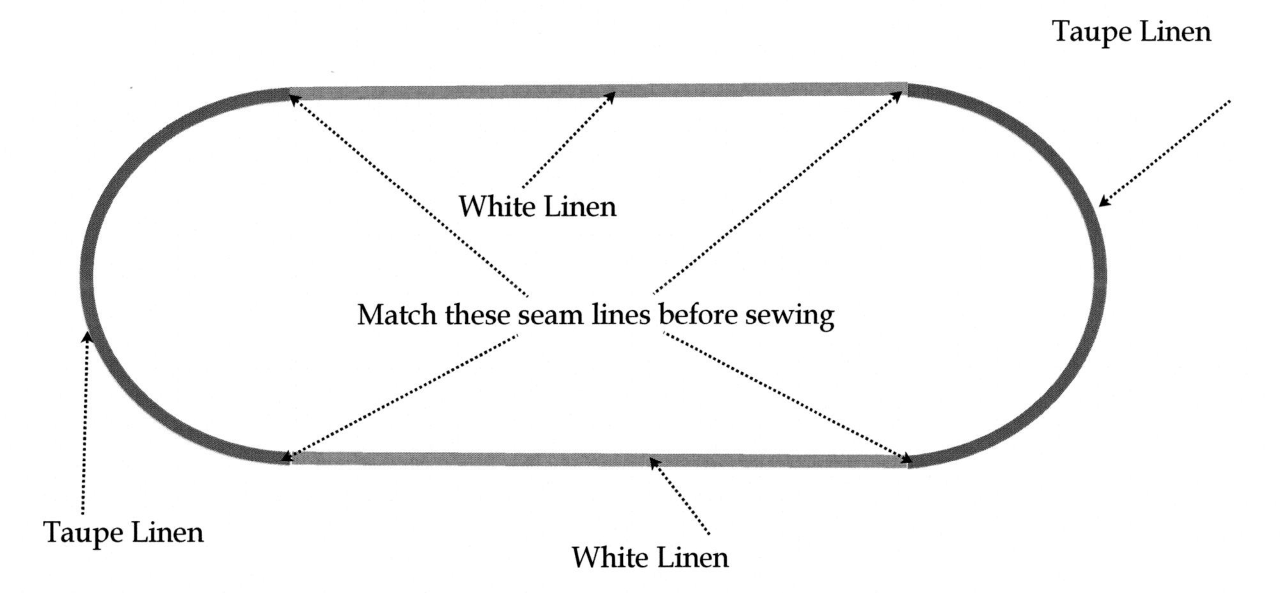

The only difference between a napkin and a table cloth is the size. Any of the designs from this book can be easily adapted to create a table cloth.

You can never go wrong by making a pure white table cloth with a hemstitched edge. Then to change the theme of your room, just change the napkins as suggested on page 51.

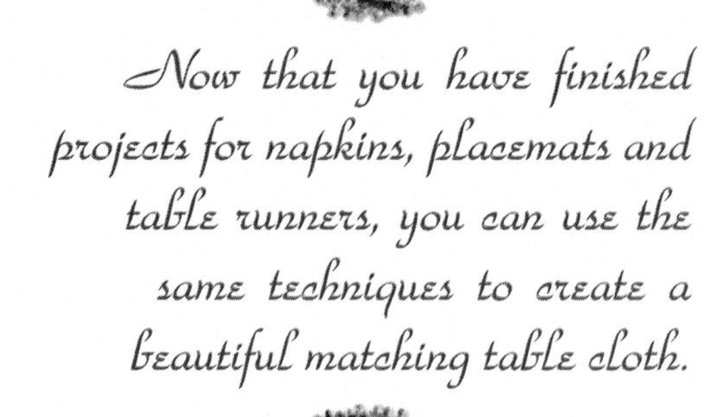

Supplies

General Supplies for Napkins and Table covers from page 47. Use the directions below to determine the yardage.

Directions

1. Measure the length of the table top. Add 10 inches for the drop—5 inches each side.
2. Measure the width of the table top. Add 10 inches for the drop—5 inches each side.
3. For each of the hem styles add the following:
   a. Scallop hem, add 2 inches to each measurement.
   b. Lace hem, add ½ inch to each measurement.
   c. Hemstitched hem, add 6 inches to each measurement.
4. Calculate the yardage you need based on the above measurements. For example, if your table top is 42 x 48 inches, and you want to hemstitch, you would need a piece of linen that is 58 by 64 inches. Since most linen comes in 60 inch widths, you would need 1 7/8 yards of linen (64 divided by 36).
5. If your table is wider that 42 inches do the following:
   a. Double the required yardage.
   b. Cut two pieces of linen to length.
   c. Cut one of the two pieces of linen in half lengthwise.
   d. If you have a serger, serge the two lengthwise pieces to the lengthwise sides of the two remaining pieces. If you do not have a serger, sew the pieces together and finish the raw edges.
   e. Press the seams.
   f. Fold the cloth in half so you have a lengthwise fold. Match the seams together so you keep on grain.
   g. Measure one half the width of the table cloth from the fold out past the seams to the edge.
   h. Cut the width of the cloth.
6. Follow the instructions for the design you want to use from the sections for towels, napkins, placemats, etc.

You may want a different drop for your table cloth. Adjust the measurements to accommodate any length of drop.

This table topper looks complicated, but it isn't. It uses a simple square lace-shaping technique above the hem and around the center embroidery. A lace edged hem finishes the edges. These are techniques that by now are very familiar to you.

This topper is made of white Swiss batiste. It is a perfect topper for a round side table or set on top of a small table in the garden to serve lemonade and cookies. The lovely embroidery on the corners and in the center is included on your CD.

Supplies

- Pansy designs from the CD or a design of your choice
- 1 ¼ yards white Swiss Batiste
- 7 yards 5/8 inch white insertion lace
- 5 ½ yards 1 ½ inch white edging lace
- White 60 weight cotton thread
- Size 70 universal needle
- Size 100 topstitching needle
- 3 inch paper stabilizer
- Tear-away stabilizer
- Blue wash-away marker
- Sulky 40 weight Rayon embroidery thread in the following colors:
  1. 1213 Dusty Lavender
  2. 1064 Light Pink
  3. 1165 Light Blue
  4. 11211 Dusty Green
  5. 11670 Brown

Directions

1. Cut the fabric into a 45 inch square.
2. Fold the fabric into quarters to find the center point.
3. Measure 12 5/8 inches from the center on all 4 sides and make a mark.
4. Draw a square around the center that is 12 5/8 inches. This is the outer line for your lace shaping (see the diagram on the next page).

When pin stitching on batiste, you want the holes to be delicate looking as shown to the left. Use a size 100 topstitching needle and a 2.5 x 2.5 stitch size for the pin stitching.

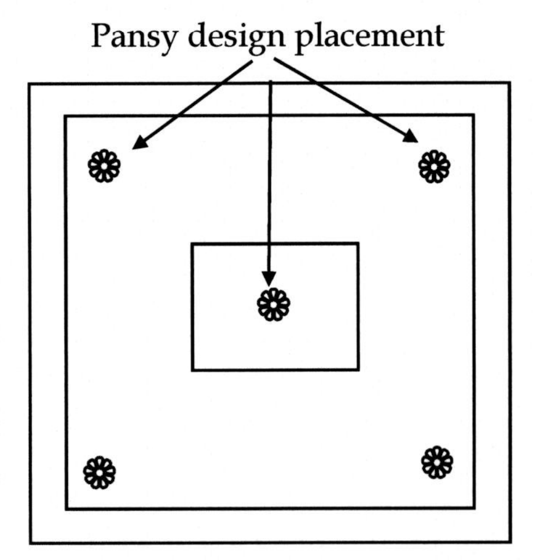

There will be a 12 inch lace square in the center of the topper with another lace square 3 inches from the sides. The pansy design goes in all four corners. As an option, you may place a design in the center of the 12 inch square.

5. Following the directions on page 33 for shaping the lace along this line to create a 12 inch square. You will be sewing on both sides of the lace.
6. Measure up 3 1/8 inches from the outer edge all the way around the fabric. This is the outer line for the lace shaping (see the above diagram).

7. Follow the directions on page 33 for shaping the lace along this line to create another square.
8. Hoop the cloth and tear away stabilizer. Embroider the design on all 4 corners and as shown in the diagram above.
9. Remove the stabilizer.
10. Follow the directions on page 25 to create a lace-edged hem.

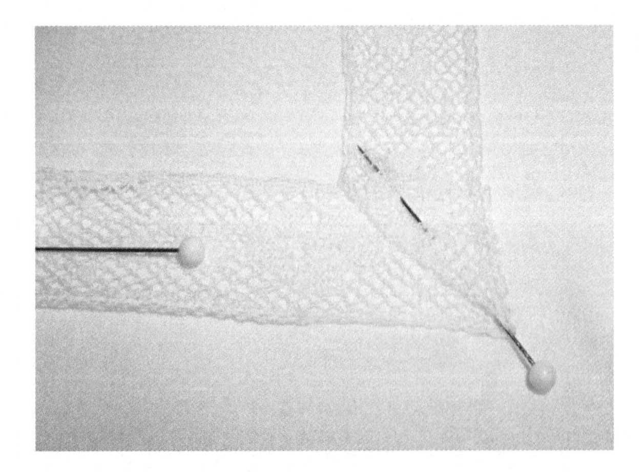

When shaping the lace, you only need to miter the corners and hold the straight areas down with a pin.

There are always scraps of fabric left over from projects you never want to throw away because they are too large to discard, but not quite big enough for much else. Below are some ideas for using your scraps. Most of these projects are made with leftover fabrics from the projects in this book.

Pretty Pot Holders

Who says pot holders have to be dull and uninteresting? These will never have to be hidden away in a drawer. Leave them on your counter by the stove or hang them on a cup hook under the cupboards.

Supplies

- 2 Scraps of white linen at least 10 inches square
- 1 10 inch scrap of white cotton fabric
- 2 10 inch scraps of ecru insertion lace
- 1 yard of white or ecru bias tape
- 1 10 inch scrap of cotton batting
- Size 120 wing needle
- Size 75 sewing needle
- 30 weight ecru Rayon thread
- Ecru or white 60 weight cotton thread

Directions

1. Fold one piece of 10 inch linen into quarters to find the center.
2. Embroider a monogram in the center of this piece.
3. Measure 2 inches from the center of this piece of linen.
4. Place the ecru lace on each size and follow the instructions for lace shaping on page 33. You will be sewing straight on both sides of the lace.
5. Stack the pieces of fabric as follows:
   - Batting.
   - Cotton piece right side up.
   - Linen & lace piece right side up.
6. Using the 60 weight cotton thread, sew a seam on each side of the lace to quilt the item.
7. Using a rotary cutter, cut this piece and the backing piece to 8½ inches square.
8. Use a small juice glass as a template draw a round shape at each corner.
9. Sew the piping to the upper piece following the round shape you made in step 8.
10. Add the backing fabric and sew around the piece leaving 2 inches on one side for turning.
11. Turn right side out and hand stitch the opening.
12. If you want to hang these from a hook, sew a small piece of bias tape into one corner.

Rose and Scallops Tiebacks

Lace curtains blowing slightly in a breeze are the epitome of a romantic look in the kitchen or dining room. Leave them loose in the spring and summer, but when the days grow cool, let the light stream in by tying them back with these beautiful tiebacks.

Supplies

- 1/4 yard white handkerchief linen
- 30 weight white Rayon thread - lavender
- Size 75 universal needle
- 3 18 inch pieces of 24 weight wire
- Hot glue gun and hot glue

Directions

1. Cut 2 pieces of linen into a strip 4½ inches by 24 inches making sure to keep on grain (see general directions).
2. Place one piece on top of the other with *wrong* sides together.
3. Starting in the center of the piece, sew three rows of decorative stitching down all 24 inches of the piece.
4. Sew a scallop stitch around the edges of the piece.
5. Sew a button hole on each end of the piece so you can attach it to a hook on the wall by the curtain edge.
6. From the scraps of linen, cut three pieces 4 inches by 18 inches.
7. Fold the piece in half lengthwise and press.
8. If you have a serger, serge a 3 thread rolled edge over the piece of wire. Press the piece and continue from step 12.
9. If you do not have a serger, sew a seam about ¼ inch from the edge creating a piece that is 2 inches by 18 inches.
10. Place a piece of wire in the seam allowance and sew it down with a zigzag stitch. Be careful not to hit the wire with your needle. The zigzag should encase the wire.
11. Turn the piece right side out and press.
12. Sew a basting stitch (L=5.0) about ¼ inch along the fold line.
13. Gently pull the basting thread to create a rose shape, turning as you pull.
14. Tack the rose in place by sewing it or use hot glue to hold it in place.
15. Hand sew or hot glue the rose onto the tie back around the button hole on one side. This will hide your hooks holding the tie back.

Coasters with a Romantic Flair

You can never have enough coasters. These tiny treasures add an elegant touch to your dinner table or they can be used anywhere in the house where you might set a glass. They make quick and easy gifts.

Supplies

- Two scraps of linen at least 6 inches square
- Monogram design from the CD in this book
- 6 inch square tear-away stabilizer
- 60 weight sewing thread
- 40 weight embroidery thread in the colors of your choice
- Size 120 wing needle.

Directions

1. Cut two 6 inch squares for each coaster.
2. Fold one square into quarters to find the center point.
3. Embroider the monogram in the center of the square using the cut-away stabilizer.
4. Place the other 6 inch square on *top* of the embroidered square, right sides together.
5. Sew around all four sides leaving a 3 inch opening on one side.
6. Turn the coaster inside out through the 3 inch opening.
7. Press well, turning under the 3 inch opening and securing it with double stick fusible tape.
8. Using a wing needle and an entredeux stitch or a reinforced straight stitch, stitch all the way around the coaster using your presser foot as a guide along the edge.

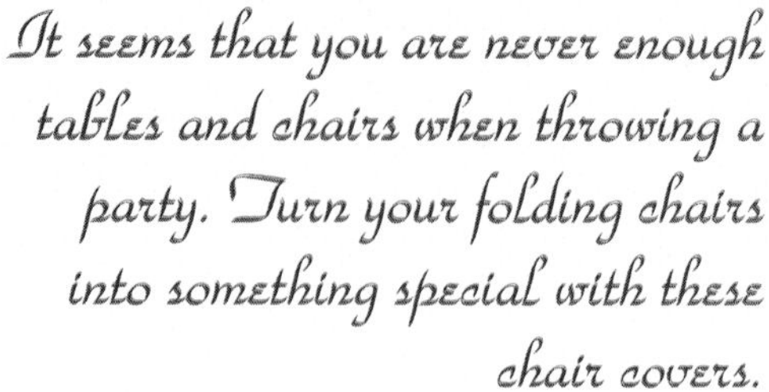

Folding Chair Covers

You can set a beautiful table using "temporary furniture." Top your plain folding chairs with these covers. Then add a table cloth for your folding table following the directions on page 60 or 61.

Supplies

- 2 pieces heavyweight linen 20 by 15 inches
- 18 inches of ¼ inch piping (or make your own from linen scraps)
- 2 pieces heavy cut away stabilizer (this will remain in the cover)
- 30 weight taupe Rayon thread
- Temporary spray adhesive
- Craft paper

Directions

1. Spray the stabilizer with the temporary spray adhesive. Place the linen fabric on top right side up on the stabilizer.
2. Sew a scallop along one 20 inch edge of both pieces of fabric.
3. Above the scallops, add embroidery, decorative stitches, eyelets or any other decoration that you would like.
4. Use a piece of craft paper to create a pattern for the top of your folding chair. Draw around the edges where the top of the chair curves.
5. Add ½ inch seam allowance to the pattern you drew in step 4. Add lines straight down the sides so your finished length will be 12-14 inches depending on the length of the metal back of your chair.
6. Cut out your linen using your chair pattern.
7. With seam allowances together, sew the piping onto one piece of the linen from the bottom around the curves to the other side.
8. Place the other piece onto the piece you sewed in step 7, right sides together.
9. Sew both pieces together. It is helpful to sew from the wrong side of the first piece so you can follow your seam line exactly.
10. Turn the piece right side out and press. Do not remove the stabilizer.

Kits

Every project in this book may be ordered as a kit. The kits include everything you need to finish the project—needles, stabilizer, fabric, thread and laces as applicable. The embroidery designs are included on the CD in this book therefore, are not included in the kits.

To order kits from this book contact:

Sew Timeless
25422 Trabuco Road, Suite 105-180
Lake Forest, CA 92630
(949) 597-1994
www.SewTimeless.com

Embroidery Designs

All embroidery designs for the projects in this book are on the CD on the last page of the book. Designs that were used for other examples come from the following companies:

Husqvarna Viking
VSM Sewing Inc.
31000 Viking Parkway
Westlake, Ohio 44145
(800) 358-0001
www.husqvarnaviking.com

Ann the Gran
Internet only
www.annthegran.com

Betsy's Wine Country Designs
Internet only
betsy@winecountrydesigns.com

Lace and Fabric

All of the companies below have a good selection of laces, linen and batiste.

Chadwick Heirlooms
5805 Grove Avenue,
Richmond, Virginia 23226
(804) 285-3355
www.chadwickheirlooms.com

Heirlooms Forever
3112 Cliff Gookin Blvd
Tupelo, Mississippi 38801
(800) 840-4275
www.sews.com

Baltazor Fabric Boutique LLC.
P.O.Box 8116
Metairie, LA 70011-8116
(504) 832-0101
www.baltazor.com

Martha Pullen Company
149 Old Big Cove Road
Brownsboro, AL 35741
(800) 547-4176

Sew Timeless
25422 Trabuco Road, Suite 105-180
Lake Forest, CA 92630
(949) 597-1994
www.SewTimeless.com

Notions

All of the companies below sell a variety of notions and sewing supplies.

Martha Pullen Company
149 Old Big Cove Road
Brownsboro, AL 35741
(800) 547-4176
www.marthapullen.com

Baltazor Fabric Boutique LLC.
P.O.Box 8116
Metairie, LA 70011-8116
(504) 832 - 0101
www.baltazor.com

Clotilde, LLC
PO Box 7500
Big Sandy, TX 75755-7500
(800) 772-2891
www.clotilde.com

The Sewing Place
PO Box 18923
Reno, NV 89511
(775) 853-3150
www.thesewingplace.com

Nancy's Notions
333 Beichl Ave.
P O Box 683
Beaver Dam, WI 53916-0683
(800) 245-5116
www.nancysnotions.com

JoAnns
(stores all over the US)
www.joanns.com

Sew Timeless
25422 Trabuco Road, Suite 105-180
Lake Forest, CA 92630
(949) 597-1994
www.SewTimeless.com

Images

Dover Publications, Inc.
31 East 2nd St.
Mineola, NY 11501
www.doverpublications.com

Madeira Towel Template

Draw the solid line for the hem.

The dotted lines help with placement
for repeating scallops.

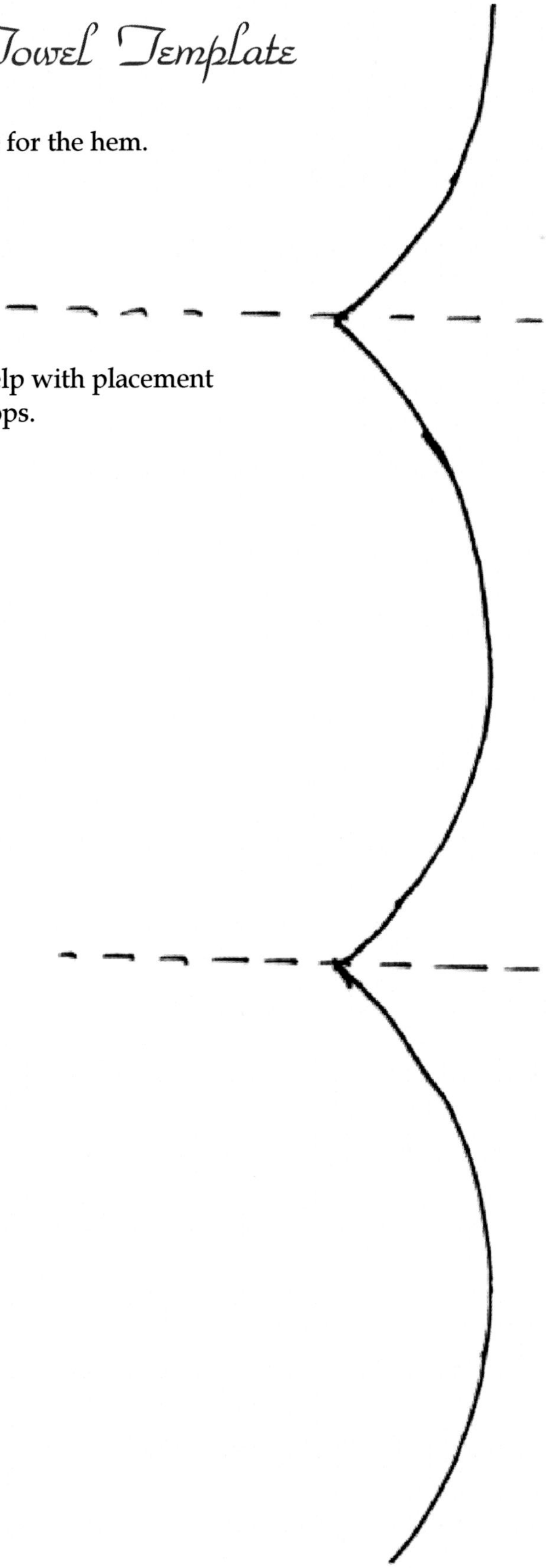

Placemat Template

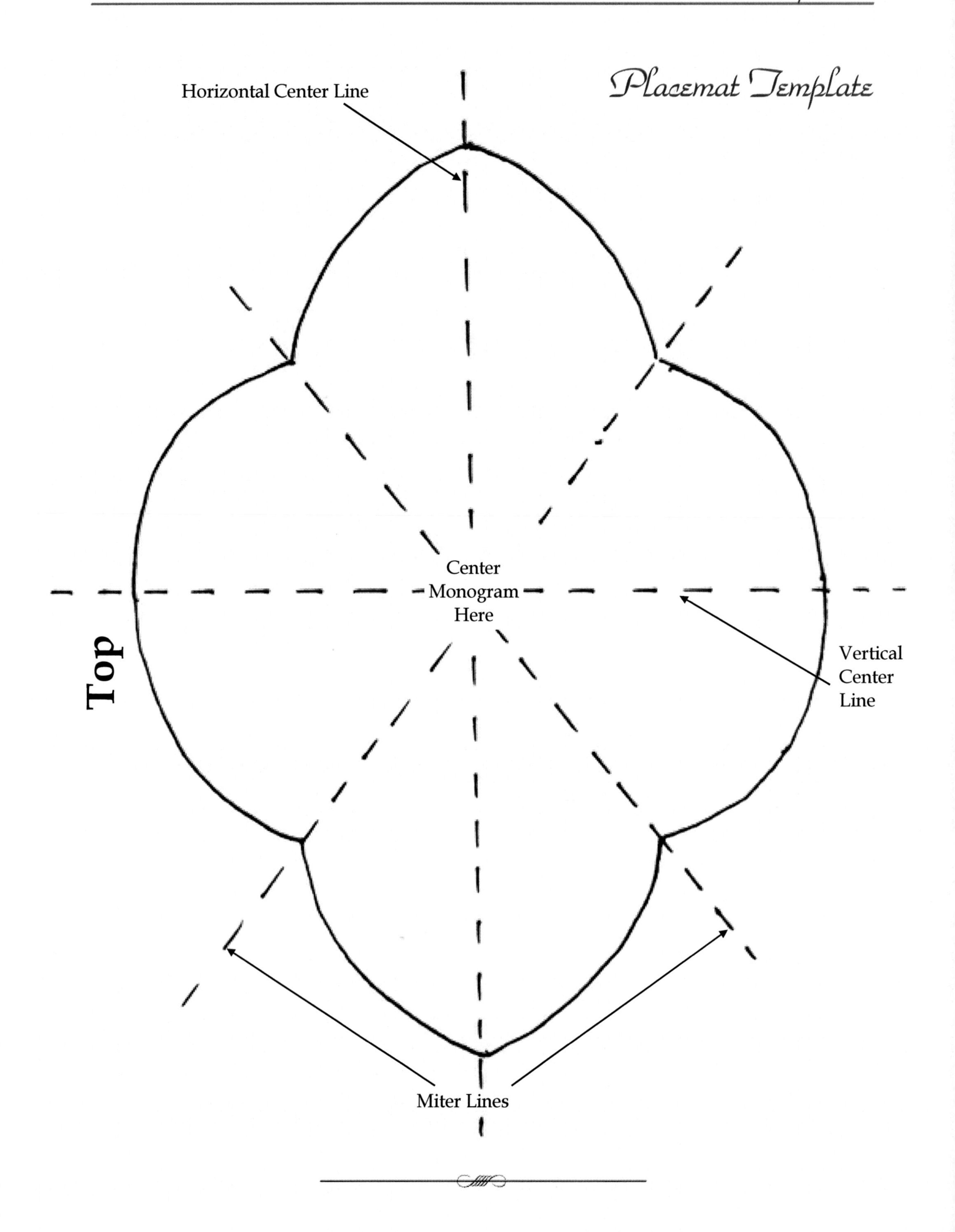

Table Runner End Template

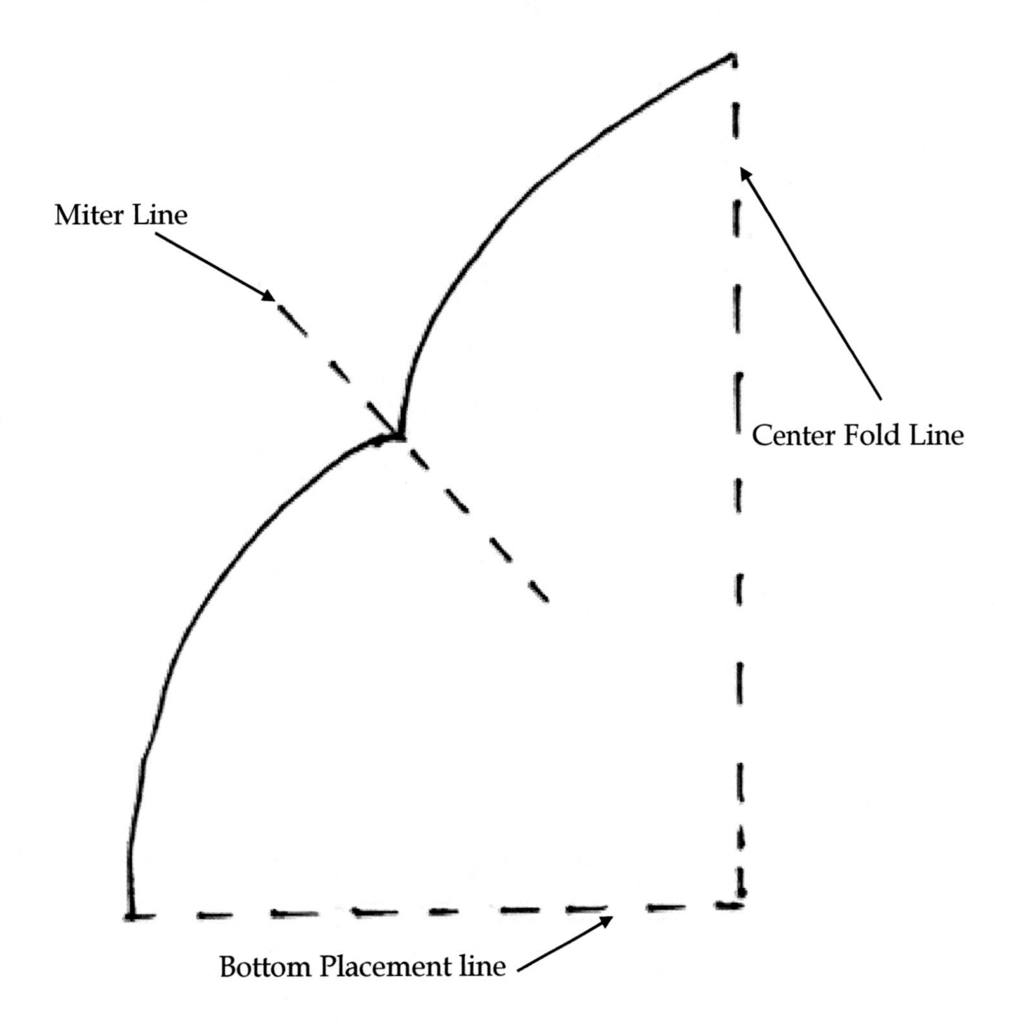

Table Runner Center Template

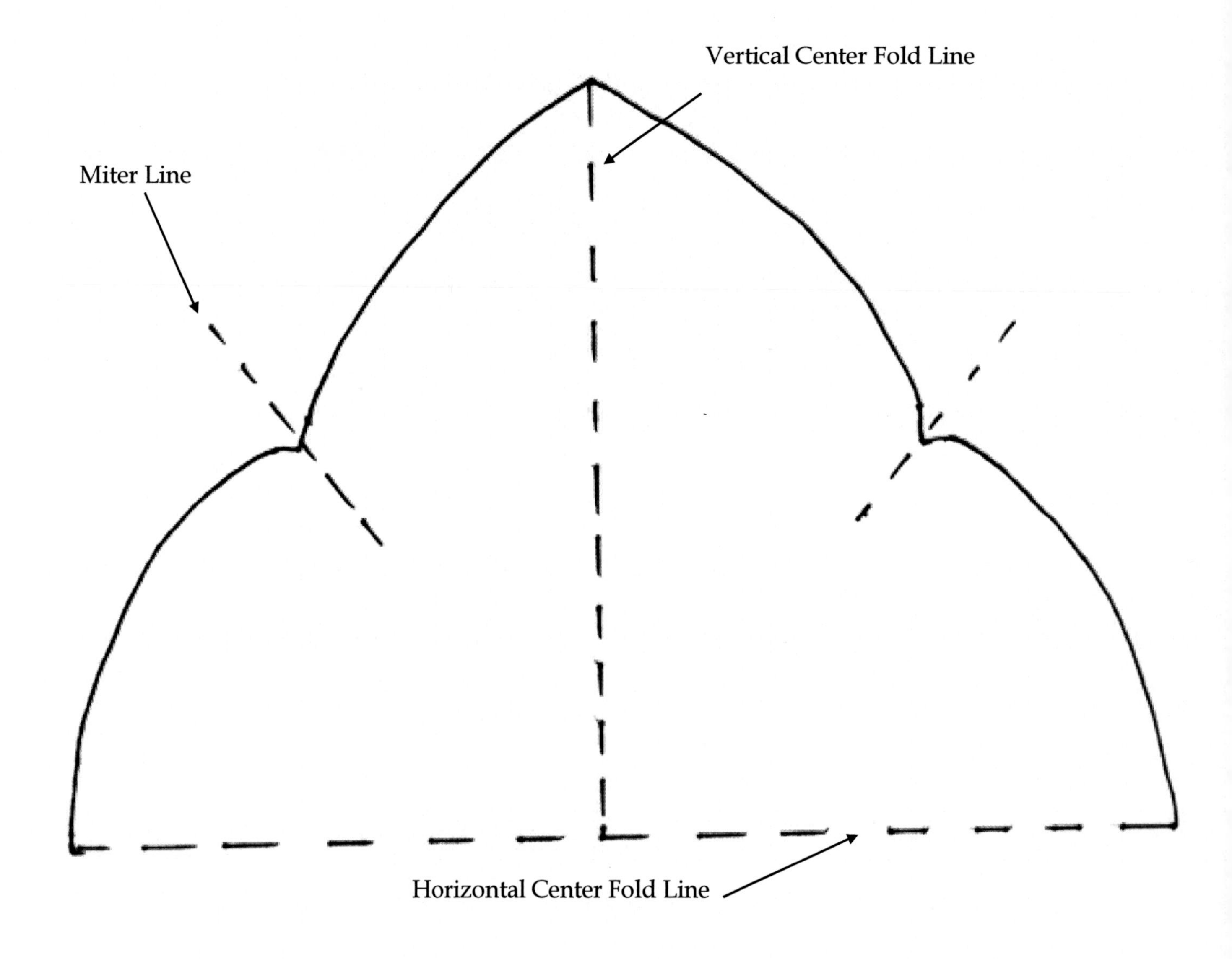

Runner Gimp Template

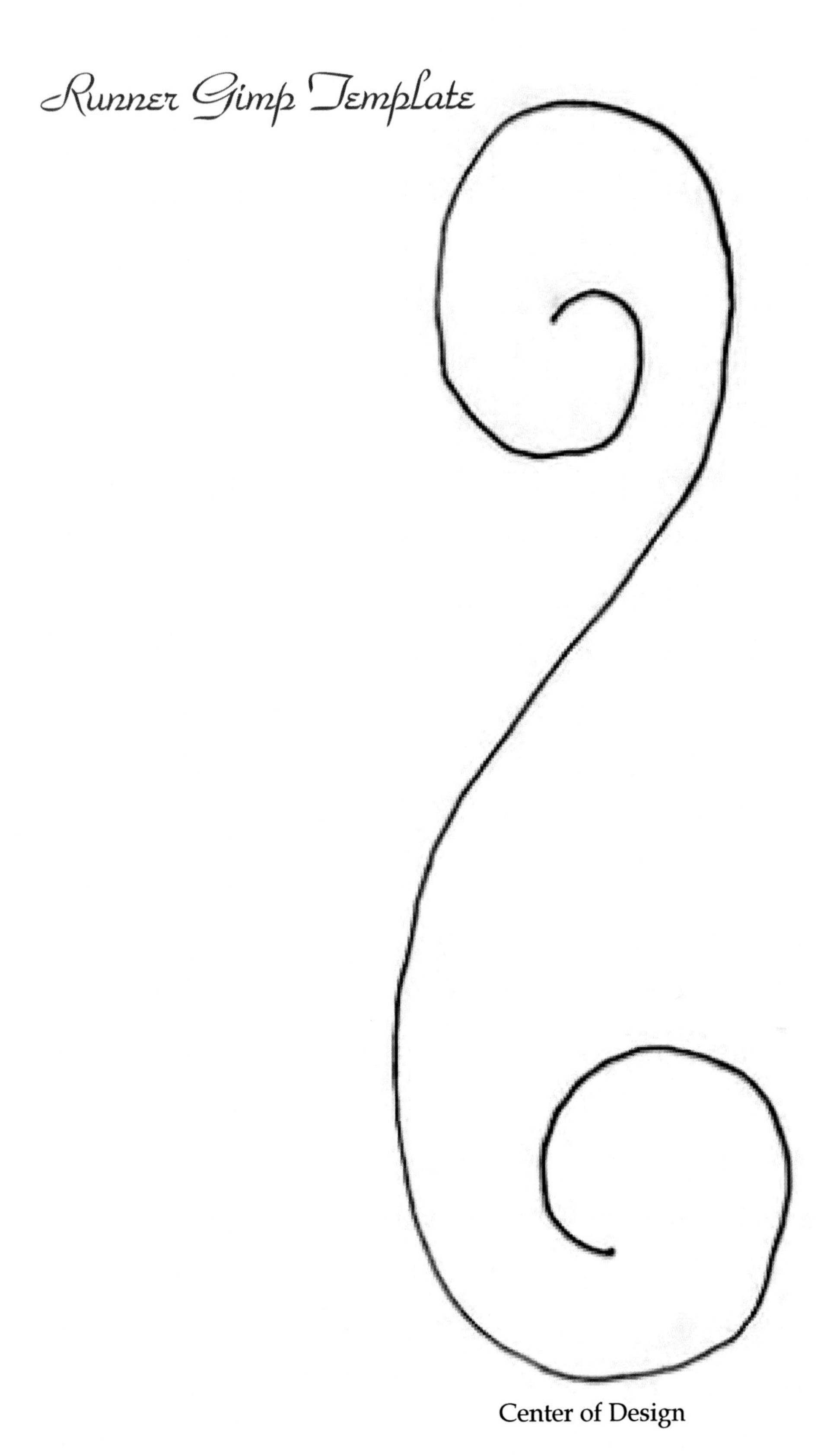

Center of Design

Place two templates together with this end in center of cloth. Use photo in the project directions as a guide.

Bottle Tag

<u>Tonight</u> I carry
a bottle of wine to enjoy
with our meal.

<u>Tomorrow</u>, take out
my basting stitches
and you'll have a
keepsake towel.

<u>Thereafter</u>, you'll have
a lasting memory of this
great evening of
food, laughter and joy
with good friends.

All of the designs and alphabets on the following pages are on the CD included with this book. The seasonal designs come both with, and without, the season name. You may use the alphabets included on the CD to create different monograms, names or labels.

One of the designs, the pansy border (shown on page 78 and pictured on pages 18 and 28), requires additional instructions. It comes in a 4 inch and 6 inch size, both have registration marks to make multiple hooping easier.

Directions for hooping the pansy border

1. If your software prints templates, print several templates so you can decide how to place your design on the edge. If your software doesn't include a template option, stitch out the design on scrap fabric to use as a template.
2. Place your template on the edge of your fabric and mark the placement line.
3. Stitch the first design. You will notice that the design starts and ends with stitches at each corner.
4. Mark these stitches with a blue wash-away marker before you remove the item from the hoop.
5. Re-hoop the next design and line up in your embroidery machine.
6. Forward to the first stitch. If this doesn't align with the registration mark, readjust the design using your left, right, up and down arrows.
7. Advance to the beginning of the design. This should line up with the previous scallop. Repeat step 6 if necessary.

The following pages contain the stitch-out information for all the designs on the CD.

bow&wheat

Width: 90.4 mm Height:95.7 mm Stitches: 8496

Technical Information - Distance From Center

Top: -47.8 mm Bottom: 47.9 mm

Left: -45.3 mm Right: 45.1 mm

6 Colors

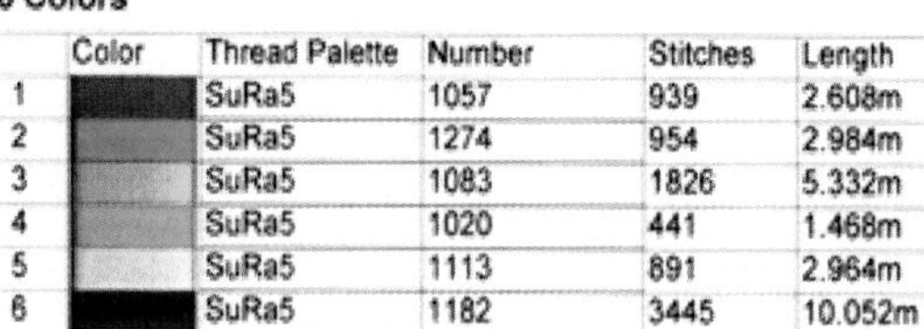

	Color	Thread Palette	Number	Stitches	Length
1		SuRa5	1057	939	2.608m
2		SuRa5	1274	954	2.984m
3		SuRa5	1083	1826	5.332m
4		SuRa5	1020	441	1.468m
5		SuRa5	1113	891	2.964m
6		SuRa5	1182	3445	10.052m

cherries

Width: 46.8 mm Height:66.5 mm Stitches: 3799

Technical Information - Distance From Center

Top: -33.1 mm Bottom: 33.4 mm

Left: -23.5 mm Right: 23.3 mm

4 Colors

	Color	Thread Palette	Number	Stitches	Length
1		SuRa5	1277	1258	4.336m
2		SuRa5	1312	525	0.783m
3		SuRa5	1184	977	3.543m
4		SuRa5	1182	1039	3.068m

flowers

Width: 90.5 mm Height:75.1 mm Stitches: 9802

Technical Information - Distance From Center

Top: -37.4 mm Bottom: 37.7 mm

Left: -44.3 mm Right: 46.2 mm

8 Colors

	Color	Thread Palette	Number	Stitches	Length
1		SuRa5	1321	1855	4.059m
2		SuRa5	1297	123	0.334m
3		SuRa5	1304	498	1.513m
4		SuRa5	1213	601	1.851m
5		SuRa5	1070	141	0.547m
6		SuRa5	1127	1719	5.066m
7		SuRa5	1291	657	1.775m
8		SuRa5	0523	4208	10.037m

flowersribbon

Width: 77.5 mm Height:97.9 mm Stitches: 7497

Technical Information - Distance From Center

Top: -48.0 mm Bottom: 49.9 mm

Left: -39.1 mm Right: 38.4 mm

9 Colors

	Color	Thread Palette	Number	Stitches	Length
1		SuRa5	1030	1425	5.356m
2		SuRa5	572	727	2.134m
3		SuRa5	1148	692	1.750m
4		SuRa5	1187	240	0.521m
5		SuRa5	1277	640	1.808m
6		SuRa5	1148	359	0.853m
7		SuRa5	1187	61	0.158m
8		SuRa5	1288	611	1.412m
9		SuRa5	1312	2742	7.422m

holley

Width: 46.1 mm Height:46.5 mm Stitches: 2343

Notes

Technical Information - Distance From Center

Top: 0.0 mm Bottom: 46.5 mm

Left: -46.1 mm Right: 0.0 mm

2 Colors

	Color	Thread Palette	Number	Stitches	Length
1		SuRa5	1263	1001	3.816m
2		SuRa5	1277	1342	2.412m

holley2

Width: 93.0 mm Height:94.1 mm Stitches: 4711

Notes

Technical Information - Distance From Center

Top: -47.0 mm Bottom: 47.1 mm

Left: -45.8 mm Right: 47.2 mm

2 Colors

	Color	Thread Palette	Number	Stitches	Length
1		SuRa5	1263	2008	7.710m
2		SuRa5	1277	2703	5.077m

Pansy4Inch

Width: 59.4 mm Height:31.6 mm Stitches: 1385

Notes

Technical Information - Distance From Center

Top: -16.1 mm Bottom: 15.5 mm

Left: -30.3 mm Right: 29.1 mm

4 Colors

	Color	Thread Palette	Number	Stitches	Length
1		SuRa5	1274	150	0.538m
2		SuRa5	1224	360	0.767m
3		SuRa5	1001	811	3.092m
4		SuRa5	1312	64	0.146m

PansyBorder

Width: 32.1 mm Height:124.2 mm Stitches: 2816

Notes

Technical Information - Distance From Center

Top: -62.1 mm Bottom: 62.1 mm

Left: -20.8 mm Right: 11.3 mm

4 Colors

	Color	Thread Palette	Number	Stitches	Length
1		SuRa5	1274	316	1.295m
2		SuRa5	1224	735	1.746m
3		SuRa5	1001	1617	6.313m
4		SuRa5	1312	148	0.572m

pansycurly

Width: 74.4 mm Height:80.5 mm Stitches: 3666

Technical Information - Distance From Center

Top: -40.2 mm Bottom: 40.3 mm

Left: -36.4 mm Right: 38.0 mm

5 Colors

	Color	Thread Palette	Number	Stitches	Length
1		SuRa5	0572	445	1.435m
2		SuRa5	1187	412	1.354m
3		SuRa5	1534	505	1.432m
4		SuRa5	1277	1801	5.615m
5		SuRa5	1182	503	1.419m

pansyheirloom

Width: 63.1 mm Height:83.0 mm Stitches: 7255

Notes

Technical Information - Distance From Center

Top: -38.6 mm Bottom: 44.4 mm

Left: -31.9 mm Right: 31.2 mm

5 Colors

	Color	Thread Palette	Number	Stitches	Length
1		SuRa5	1534	1601	5.920m
2		SuRa5	1288	1351	6.015m
3		SuRa5	1061	944	3.415m
4		SuRa5	1001	836	3.005m
5		SuRa5	1265	2523	6.668m

roses

Width: 74.3 mm Height:56.4 mm Stitches: 3046

Technical Information - Distance From Center

Top: -28.2 mm Bottom: 28.2 mm

Left: -36.3 mm Right: 38.0 mm

3 Colors

	Color	Thread Palette	Number	Stitches	Length
1		SuRa5	1274	2098	7.086m
2		SuRa5	1020	242	1.121m
3		SuRa5	1312	706	1.804m

season1

Width: 87.1 mm Height:80.5 mm Stitches: 5223

Notes

Technical Information - Distance From Center

Top: -39.5 mm Bottom: 41.0 mm

Left: -43.6 mm Right: 43.5 mm

6 Colors

	Color	Thread Palette	Number	Stitches	Length
1		SuRa5	0572	445	1.443m
2		SuRa5	1187	412	1.354m
3		SuRa5	1534	505	1.432m
4		SuRa5	1277	1800	5.614m
5		SuRa5	1182	503	1.419m
6		SuRa5	1226	1558	5.440m

season2

Width: 79.4 mm Height:77.8 mm Stitches: 5390

Notes

Technical Information - Distance From Center

Top: -44.9 mm Bottom: 32.9 mm

Left: -39.4 mm Right: 40.0 mm

5 Colors

	Color	Thread Palette	Number	Stitches	Length
1		SuRa5	1277	1259	4.349m
2		SuRa5	1312	525	0.783m
3		SuRa5	1184	977	3.543m
4		SuRa5	1182	1035	3.068m
5		SuRa5	1226	1594	5.502m

season3

Width: 72.7 mm Height:94.9 mm Stitches: 8843

Notes

Technical Information - Distance From Center

Top: -46.2 mm Bottom: 48.7 mm

Left: -35.9 mm Right: 36.8 mm

7 Colors

	Color	Thread Palette	Number	Stitches	Length
1		SuRa5	1057	809	1.945m
2		SuRa5	1274	897	2.228m
3		SuRa5	1083	1639	3.657m
4		SuRa5	1020	397	1.170m
5		SuRa5	1113	856	2.181m
6		SuRa5	1182	2053	6.934m
7		RaRa5	2469	2192	6.073m

season4

Width: 93.0 mm Height:94.1 mm Stitches: 6324

Notes

Technical Information - Distance From Center

Top: -47.0 mm Bottom: 47.1 mm

Left: -45.8 mm Right: 47.2 mm

3 Colors

	Color	Thread Palette	Number	Stitches	Length
1		SuRa5	1263	2008	7.710m
2		SuRa5	1277	2703	5.077m
3		RaRa5	2596	1613	5.631m

a

Width: 73.2 mm Height:66.7 mm Stitches: 8767

Notes

Technical Information - Distance From Center

Top: -36.8 mm Bottom: 29.9 mm

Left: -40.3 mm Right: 32.9 mm

5 Colors

	Color	Thread Palette	Number	Stitches	Length
1		SuRa5	1061	1939	9.092m
2		SuRa5	1274	1648	4.352m
3		SuRa5	1020	56	0.239m
4		SuRa5	1148	161	0.562m
5		SuRa5	1312	4963	12.523m

b

Width: 75.1 mm Height:57.5 mm Stitches: 8857

Notes

Technical Information - Distance From Center

Top: -36.3 mm Bottom: 21.2 mm

Left: -40.1 mm Right: 35.0 mm

5 Colors

	Color	Thread Palette	Number	Stitches	Length
1		SuRa5	1061	2030	10.103m
2		SuRa5	1274	1649	4.370m
3		SuRa5	1020	56	0.239m
4		SuRa5	1148	161	0.562m
5		SuRa5	1312	4961	12.570m

c

Width: 65.0 mm Height:73.7 mm Stitches: 8256

Notes

Technical Information - Distance From Center

Top: -42.7 mm Bottom: 31.0 mm

Left: -37.3 mm Right: 27.7 mm

5 Colors

	Color	Thread Palette	Number	Stitches	Length
1		SuRa5	1061	1435	7.052m
2		SuRa5	1274	1643	4.334m
3		SuRa5	1020	56	0.239m
4		SuRa5	1148	161	0.562m
5		SuRa5	1312	4961	12.556m

d

Width: 70.8 mm Height:62.8 mm Stitches: 8817

Notes

Technical Information - Distance From Center

Top: -37.5 mm Bottom: 25.3 mm

Left: -41.7 mm Right: 29.1 mm

5 Colors

	Color	Thread Palette	Number	Stitches	Length
1		SuRa5	1061	1996	10.205m
2		SuRa5	1274	1643	4.307m
3		SuRa5	1020	56	0.239m
4		SuRa5	1148	161	0.562m
5		SuRa5	1312	4961	12.533m

e

Width: 80.2 mm Height:57.2 mm Stitches: 8558

Notes

Technical Information - Distance From Center

Top: -36.4 mm Bottom: 20.8 mm

Left: -46.0 mm Right: 34.2 mm

5 Colors

	Color	Thread Palette	Number	Stitches	Length
1		SuRa5	1061	1730	8.797m
2		SuRa5	1274	1646	4.381m
3		SuRa5	1020	56	0.238m
4		SuRa5	1148	161	0.563m
5		SuRa5	1312	4965	12.557m

f

Width: 78.6 mm Height:57.9 mm Stitches: 8294

Notes

Technical Information - Distance From Center

Top: -33.6 mm Bottom: 24.3 mm

Left: -37.7 mm Right: 40.9 mm

5 Colors

	Color	Thread Palette	Number	Stitches	Length
1		SuRa5	1061	1473	7.047m
2		SuRa5	1274	1643	4.300m
3		SuRa5	1020	56	0.240m
4		SuRa5	1148	161	0.563m
5		SuRa5	1312	4961	12.531m

g

Width: 72.9 mm Height:65.3 mm Stitches: 8793

Notes

Technical Information - Distance From Center

Top: -35.9 mm Bottom: 29.4 mm

Left: -45.0 mm Right: 27.9 mm

5 Colors

	Color	Thread Palette	Number	Stitches	Length
1		SuRa5	1061	1983	10.089m
2		SuRa5	1274	1647	4.345m
3		SuRa5	1020	56	0.240m
4		SuRa5	1148	161	0.563m
5		SuRa5	1312	4946	12.542m

h

Width: 79.3 mm Height:56.8 mm Stitches: 8440

Notes

Technical Information - Distance From Center

Top: -30.5 mm Bottom: 26.3 mm

Left: -38.2 mm Right: 41.1 mm

5 Colors

	Color	Thread Palette	Number	Stitches	Length
1		SuRa5	1061	1628	7.668m
2		SuRa5	1274	1643	4.303m
3		SuRa5	1020	56	0.239m
4		SuRa5	1148	161	0.564m
5		SuRa5	1312	4952	12.533m

i

Width: 68.5 mm Height:55.1 mm Stitches: 7990

Notes

Technical Information - Distance From Center

Top: -35.0 mm Bottom: 20.1 mm

Left: -40.6 mm Right: 27.9 mm

5 Colors

	Color	Thread Palette	Number	Stitches	Length
1		SuRa5	1061	1171	5.549m
2		SuRa5	1274	1642	4.294m
3		SuRa5	1020	56	0.240m
4		SuRa5	1148	161	0.563m
5		SuRa5	1312	4960	12.552m

j

Width: 73.1 mm Height:73.7 mm Stitches: 8083

Notes

Technical Information - Distance From Center

Top: -39.5 mm Bottom: 34.2 mm

Left: -34.7 mm Right: 38.4 mm

5 Colors

	Color	Thread Palette	Number	Stitches	Length
1		SuRa5	1061	1270	5.921m
2		SuRa5	1274	1648	4.364m
3		SuRa5	1020	56	0.239m
4		SuRa5	1148	161	0.565m
5		SuRa5	1312	4948	12.511m

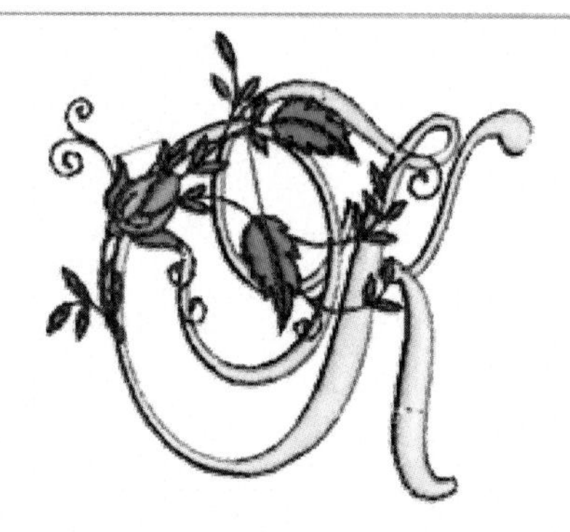

k

Width: 74.3 mm Height:70.3 mm Stitches: 8970

Notes

Technical Information - Distance From Center

Top: -39.7 mm Bottom: 30.6 mm

Left: -35.4 mm Right: 38.9 mm

5 Colors

	Color	Thread Palette	Number	Stitches	Length
1		SuRa5	1061	2147	10.494m
2		SuRa5	1274	1649	4.382m
3		SuRa5	1020	56	0.239m
4		SuRa5	1148	161	0.569m
5		SuRa5	1312	4957	12.571m

l

Width: 64.6 mm Height:64.4 mm Stitches: 8185

Notes

Technical Information - Distance From Center

Top: -39.1 mm Bottom: 25.3 mm

Left: -38.2 mm Right: 26.4 mm

5 Colors

	Color	Thread Palette	Number	Stitches	Length
1		SuRa5	1061	1369	6.931m
2		SuRa5	1274	1643	4.311m
3		SuRa5	1020	56	0.238m
4		SuRa5	1148	161	0.562m
5		SuRa5	1312	4956	12.545m

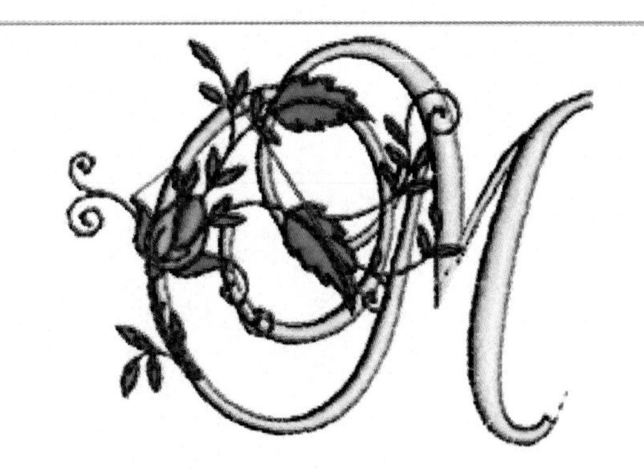

m

Width: 77.4 mm Height:58.5 mm Stitches: 8616

Notes

Technical Information - Distance From Center

Top: -37.7 mm Bottom: 20.8 mm

Left: -43.8 mm Right: 33.6 mm

5 Colors

	Color	Thread Palette	Number	Stitches	Length
1		SuRa5	1061	1794	8.133m
2		SuRa5	1274	1644	4.296m
3		SuRa5	1020	56	0.240m
4		SuRa5	1148	161	0.561m
5		SuRa5	1312	4961	12.534m

n

Width: 83.0 mm Height:60.3 mm Stitches: 8903

Notes

Technical Information - Distance From Center

Top: -34.3 mm Bottom: 26.0 mm

Left: -42.7 mm Right: 40.3 mm

5 Colors

	Color	Thread Palette	Number	Stitches	Length
1		SuRa5	1061	2091	8.674m
2		SuRa5	1274	1639	4.328m
3		SuRa5	1020	56	0.239m
4		SuRa5	1148	161	0.561m
5		SuRa5	1312	4956	12.587m

o

Width: 67.2 mm Height:72.1 mm Stitches: 8400

Notes

Technical Information - Distance From Center

Top: -43.8 mm Bottom: 28.3 mm

Left: -38.5 mm Right: 28.7 mm

5 Colors

	Color	Thread Palette	Number	Stitches	Length
1		SuRa5	1061	1586	6.988m
2		SuRa5	1274	1645	4.319m
3		SuRa5	1020	56	0.239m
4		SuRa5	1148	161	0.561m
5		SuRa5	1312	4952	12.575m

p

Width: 72.3 mm Height:68.4 mm Stitches: 8598

Notes

Technical Information - Distance From Center

Top: -42.6 mm Bottom: 25.8 mm

Left: -39.8 mm Right: 32.5 mm

5 Colors

	Color	Thread Palette	Number	Stitches	Length
1		SuRa5	1061	1801	8.583m
2		SuRa5	1274	1642	4.339m
3		SuRa5	1020	56	0.240m
4		SuRa5	1148	161	0.560m
5		SuRa5	1312	4938	12.587m

q

Width: 69.2 mm Height:78.2 mm Stitches: 8551

Notes

Technical Information - Distance From Center

Top: -46.8 mm Bottom: 31.4 mm

Left: -39.7 mm Right: 29.5 mm

5 Colors

	Color	Thread Palette	Number	Stitches	Length
1		SuRa5	1061	1725	8.042m
2		SuRa5	1274	1644	4.302m
3		SuRa5	1020	56	0.240m
4		SuRa5	1148	161	0.563m
5		SuRa5	1312	4965	12.554m

r

Width: 74.8 mm Height:67.2 mm Stitches: 8573

Notes

Technical Information - Distance From Center

Top: -39.5 mm Bottom: 27.7 mm

Left: -43.5 mm Right: 31.3 mm

5 Colors

	Color	Thread Palette	Number	Stitches	Length
1		SuRa5	1061	1755	8.548m
2		SuRa5	1274	1644	4.318m
3		SuRa5	1020	56	0.237m
4		SuRa5	1148	161	0.566m
5		SuRa5	1312	4957	12.552m

s

Width: 70.1 mm Height:61.3 mm Stitches: 8475

Notes

Technical Information - Distance From Center

Top: -39.1 mm Bottom: 22.2 mm

Left: -28.8 mm Right: 41.3 mm

5 Colors

	Color	Thread Palette	Number	Stitches	Length
1		SuRa5	1061	1652	7.845m
2		SuRa5	1274	1642	4.283m
3		SuRa5	1020	56	0.240m
4		SuRa5	1148	161	0.563m
5		SuRa5	1312	4964	12.539m

t

Width: 78.0 mm Height:59.0 mm Stitches: 8270

Notes

Technical Information - Distance From Center

Top: -37.6 mm Bottom: 21.4 mm

Left: -41.6 mm Right: 36.4 mm

5 Colors

	Color	Thread Palette	Number	Stitches	Length
1		SuRa5	1061	1455	6.964m
2		SuRa5	1274	1640	4.296m
3		SuRa5	1020	56	0.240m
4		SuRa5	1148	161	0.564m
5		SuRa5	1312	4958	12.544m

u

Width: 78.5 mm Height:65.1 mm Stitches: 7964

Notes

Technical Information - Distance From Center

Top: -42.6 mm Bottom: 22.5 mm

Left: -44.3 mm Right: 34.2 mm

5 Colors

	Color	Thread Palette	Number	Stitches	Length
1		SuRa5	1061	1141	6.218m
2		SuRa5	1274	1644	4.314m
3		SuRa5	1020	56	0.239m
4		SuRa5	1148	161	0.561m
5		SuRa5	1312	4962	12.566m

v

Width: 81.7 mm Height:68.4 mm Stitches: 8028

Notes

Technical Information - Distance From Center

Top: -35.9 mm Bottom: 32.5 mm

Left: -43.1 mm Right: 38.6 mm

5 Colors

	Color	Thread Palette	Number	Stitches	Length
1		SuRa5	1061	1204	5.446m
2		SuRa5	1274	1645	4.324m
3		SuRa5	1020	56	0.240m
4		SuRa5	1148	161	0.565m
5		SuRa5	1312	4962	12.560m

w

Width: 89.0 mm Height:72.1 mm Stitches: 8371

Notes

Technical Information - Distance From Center

Top: -47.2 mm Bottom: 24.9 mm

Left: -46.4 mm Right: 42.6 mm

5 Colors

	Color	Thread Palette	Number	Stitches	Length
1		SuRa5	1061	1551	7.066m
2		SuRa5	1274	1644	4.310m
3		SuRa5	1020	56	0.239m
4		SuRa5	1148	161	0.563m
5		SuRa5	1312	4959	12.567m

x

Width: 78.6 mm Height:58.7 mm Stitches: 8368

Notes

Technical Information - Distance From Center

Top: -39.4 mm Bottom: 19.3 mm

Left: -39.8 mm Right: 38.8 mm

5 Colors

	Color	Thread Palette	Number	Stitches	Length
1		SuRa5	1061	1548	6.601m
2		SuRa5	1274	1644	4.303m
3		SuRa5	1020	56	0.240m
4		SuRa5	1148	161	0.565m
5		SuRa5	1312	4959	12.564m

y

Width: 73.5 mm Height:67.6 mm Stitches: 8089

Notes

Technical Information - Distance From Center

Top: -39.8 mm Bottom: 27.8 mm

Left: -40.7 mm Right: 32.8 mm

5 Colors

	Color	Thread Palette	Number	Stitches	Length
1		SuRa5	1061	1280	6.509m
2		SuRa5	1274	1642	4.322m
3		SuRa5	1020	56	0.240m
4		SuRa5	1148	161	0.563m
5		SuRa5	1312	4950	12.555m

z.vip - C:\embroidery\digitize\alpha2

Width: 77.6 mm Height:63.8 mm Stitches: 8267

Notes

Technical Information - Distance From Center

Top: -37.5 mm Bottom: 26.3 mm

Left: -42.6 mm Right: 35.0 mm

5 Colors

	Color	Thread Palette	Number	Stitches	Length
1		SuRa5	1061	1445	7.529m
2		SuRa5	1274	1643	4.306m
3		SuRa5	1020	56	0.238m
4		SuRa5	1148	161	0.562m
5		SuRa5	1312	4962	12.548m

038_& Width: 35.6 mm Height:44.6 mm Stitches: 760	045_- Width: 24.7 mm Height:21.7 mm Stitches: 136	048_0 Width: 27.1 mm Height:43.6 mm Stitches: 509	049_1 Width: 17.4 mm Height:40.6 mm Stitches: 316
050_2 Width: 27.1 mm Height:41.4 mm Stitches: 519	051_3 Width: 27.1 mm Height:41.4 mm Stitches: 518	052_4 Width: 31.1 mm Height:41.6 mm Stitches: 608	053_5 Width: 27.5 mm Height:42.3 mm Stitches: 543
054_6 Width: 27.1 mm Height:42.0 mm Stitches: 596	055_7 Width: 28.6 mm Height:42.1 mm Stitches: 418	056_8 Width: 27.1 mm Height:43.2 mm Stitches: 636	057_9 Width: 27.1 mm Height:42.1 mm Stitches: 534
065_A_UC Width: 38.0 mm Height:49.9 mm Stitches: 723	066_B_UC Width: 35.5 mm Height:51.1 mm Stitches: 1091	067_C_UC Width: 40.1 mm Height:50.1 mm Stitches: 915	068_D_UC Width: 39.7 mm Height:48.6 mm Stitches: 930
069_E_UC Width: 33.6 mm Height:50.1 mm Stitches: 978	070_F_UC Width: 49.5 mm Height:54.4 mm Stitches: 1020	071_G_UC Width: 44.3 mm Height:50.3 mm Stitches: 1088	072_H_UC Width: 43.7 mm Height:47.4 mm Stitches: 1212
073_I_UC Width: 29.5 mm Height:52.0 mm Stitches: 850	074_J_UC Width: 29.2 mm Height:53.3 mm Stitches: 911	075_K_UC Width: 48.1 mm Height:46.7 mm Stitches: 972	076_L_UC Width: 33.1 mm Height:51.5 mm Stitches: 749
077_M_UC Width: 53.4 mm Height:46.2 mm Stitches: 1412	078_N_UC Width: 44.1 mm Height:48.8 mm Stitches: 1023	079_O_UC Width: 46.9 mm Height:51.2 mm Stitches: 944	080_P_UC Width: 32.2 mm Height:50.3 mm Stitches: 896
081_Q_UC Width: 47.4 mm Height:53.8 mm Stitches: 1166	082_R_UC Width: 37.5 mm Height:50.4 mm Stitches: 1097	083_S_UC Width: 34.2 mm Height:54.8 mm Stitches: 922	084_T_UC Width: 49.5 mm Height:52.8 mm Stitches: 1096

 085_U_UC Width: 54.7 mm Height:51.7 mm Stitches: 1232	 086_V_UC Width: 43.2 mm Height:49.2 mm Stitches: 985	 087_W_UC Width: 55.6 mm Height:51.7 mm Stitches: 1305	 088_X_UC.vip Width: 43.5 mm Height:48.5 mm Stitches: 912 C:\embroidery\alpha\CAC Valiant_R_50\Stitch
 089_Y_UC Width: 55.4 mm Height:61.7 mm Stitches: 1109	 090_Z_UC Width: 39.1 mm Height:50.2 mm Stitches: 1133	 097_a Width: 25.6 mm Height:35.0 mm Stitches: 554	 098_b.vip Width: 26.2 mm Height:51.9 mm Stitches: 642 C:\embroidery\alpha\CAC Valiant_R_50\Stitch
 099_c Width: 20.9 mm Height:34.8 mm Stitches: 348	 100_d Width: 24.1 mm Height:53.2 mm Stitches: 599	 101_e Width: 20.1 mm Height:35.8 mm Stitches: 420	 102_f.vip Width: 33.9 mm Height:64.0 mm Stitches: 527 C:\embroidery\alpha\CAC Valiant_R_50\Stitch
 103_g Width: 25.8 mm Height:49.2 mm Stitches: 659	 104_h Width: 29.6 mm Height:51.4 mm Stitches: 621	 105_i Width: 15.2 mm Height:47.4 mm Stitches: 301	 106_j.vip Width: 19.1 mm Height:56.3 mm Stitches: 413 C:\embroidery\alpha\CAC Valiant_R_50\Stitch
 107_k Width: 26.7 mm Height:50.9 mm Stitches: 681	 108_l Width: 17.8 mm Height:52.7 mm Stitches: 352	 109_m Width: 39.5 mm Height:34.5 mm Stitches: 679	 110_n.vip Width: 27.6 mm Height:34.8 mm Stitches: 501 C:\embroidery\alpha\CAC Valiant_R_50\Stitch
 111_o Width: 22.1 mm Height:35.7 mm Stitches: 420	 112_p Width: 33.9 mm Height:50.8 mm Stitches: 699	 113_q Width: 31.9 mm Height:47.0 mm Stitches: 636	 114_r.vip Width: 21.2 mm Height:35.0 mm Stitches: 321 C:\embroidery\alpha\CAC Valiant_R_50\Stitch
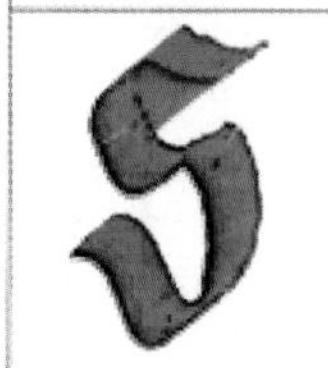 115_s Width: 23.7 mm Height:35.2 mm Stitches: 506	 116_t Width: 16.5 mm Height:40.7 mm Stitches: 337	 117_u Width: 30.6 mm Height:35.3 mm Stitches: 449	 118_v.vip Width: 25.9 mm Height:34.6 mm Stitches: 424
 119_w Width: 38.5 mm Height:35.2 mm Stitches: 602	 120_x Width: 29.2 mm Height:35.6 mm Stitches: 699	 121_y Width: 28.7 mm Height:49.1 mm Stitches: 661	 122_z Width: 26.1 mm Height:35.8 mm Stitches: 613

048_0 Width: 28.5 mm Height:33.9 mm Stitches: 442	049_1 Width: 24.9 mm Height:32.8 mm Stitches: 290	050_2 Width: 29.1 mm Height:33.7 mm Stitches: 580	051_3 Width: 28.6 mm Height:33.7 mm Stitches: 522
052_4 Width: 26.9 mm Height:32.3 mm Stitches: 403	053_5 Width: 30.7 mm Height:33.7 mm Stitches: 468	054_6 Width: 33.3 mm Height:33.9 mm Stitches: 472	055_7 Width: 29.8 mm Height:33.6 mm Stitches: 332
056_8 Width: 28.2 mm Height:33.8 mm Stitches: 499	057_9 Width: 29.6 mm Height:33.7 mm Stitches: 504	063 Width: 25.2 mm Height:34.4 mm Stitches: 330	064_@ Width: 66.4 mm Height:57.7 mm Stitches: 1313
065_A_UC Width: 97.0 mm Height:49.8 mm Stitches: 1632	066_B_UC Width: 70.4 mm Height:52.2 mm Stitches: 1654	067_C_UC Width: 63.3 mm Height:57.1 mm Stitches: 1336	068_D_UC Width: 63.3 mm Height:51.1 mm Stitches: 1488
069_E_UC Width: 48.6 mm Height:57.2 mm Stitches: 1291	070_F_UC Width: 91.4 mm Height:49.6 mm Stitches: 1663	071_G_UC Width: 76.6 mm Height:62.6 mm Stitches: 1779	072_H_UC Width: 101.9 mm Height:49.4 mm Stitches: 1867
073_I_UC Width: 79.5 mm Height:48.5 mm Stitches: 1186	074_J_UC Width: 81.9 mm Height:71.1 mm Stitches: 1551	075_K_UC Width: 101.5 mm Height:49.0 mm Stitches: 1632	076_L_UC Width: 64.1 mm Height:50.7 mm Stitches: 1190
077_M_UC Width: 97.0 mm Height:48.6 mm Stitches: 1850	078_N_UC Width: 100.4 mm Height:48.9 mm Stitches: 1249	079_O_UC Width: 55.9 mm Height:50.2 mm Stitches: 1391	080_P_UC Width: 68.6 mm Height:50.7 mm Stitches: 1351
081_Q_UC Width: 56.7 mm Height:50.7 mm Stitches: 1315	082_R_UC Width: 68.3 mm Height:51.1 mm Stitches: 1489	083_S_UC Width: 74.9 mm Height:50.7 mm Stitches: 1341	084_T_UC Width: 90.0 mm Height:49.2 mm Stitches: 1429

Design	Width	Height	Stitches
085_U_UC	73.5 mm	49.8 mm	1257
086_V_UC	73.7 mm	50.8 mm	1122
087_W_UC	90.8 mm	50.7 mm	1689
088_X_UC	70.0 mm	49.9 mm	1623
089_Y_UC	84.4 mm	58.3 mm	1557
090_Z_UC	70.1 mm	49.7 mm	1290
097_a	28.0 mm	20.3 mm	423
098_b	26.5 mm	41.7 mm	446
099_c	20.3 mm	20.3 mm	306
100_d	38.5 mm	41.9 mm	557
101_e	20.7 mm	20.3 mm	336
102_f	44.3 mm	62.0 mm	660
103_g	33.6 mm	41.1 mm	717
104_h	29.7 mm	41.9 mm	611
105_i	20.1 mm	33.1 mm	291
106_j	36.2 mm	54.2 mm	603
107_k	30.2 mm	41.8 mm	596
108_l	27.8 mm	41.9 mm	355
109_m	43.0 mm	20.4 mm	719
110_n	31.5 mm	20.3 mm	495
111_o	24.7 mm	20.1 mm	352
112_p	39.7 mm	49.9 mm	629
113_q	26.9 mm	38.6 mm	583
114_r	24.3 mm	19.6 mm	355
115_s	17.9 mm	22.6 mm	288
116_t	25.7 mm	32.9 mm	429
117_u	27.8 mm	19.6 mm	435
118_v	29.2 mm	20.0 mm	429
119_w	36.7 mm	19.8 mm	485
120_x	29.4 mm	20.6 mm	438
121_y	33.8 mm	41.2 mm	751
122_z	25.8 mm	20.0 mm	458

C:\embroidery\alpha\ShelleyAllegro B...\Stitch

25422 Trabuco Road
Suite 105-180
Lake Forest, CA 92630
(949) 597-1994
www.SewTimeless.com

Kit Order Form

Sewing for the Romantic Home / Volume 1

Product No.	Item	Price Per Unit	Number of Units	Extended Price
RH100	Hemstitched Pansy Towel Kit	$24.00		
RH110	Muted Flowers Madeira Towel Kit	$30.00		
RH120	Victorian Monogrammed Lace Towel Kit	$35.00		
RH130	Formal Dinner Napkins Kit (makes 2)	$20.00		
RH140	Pretty Luncheon Napkins Kit (makes 2)	$30.00		
RH150	Napkins for All Seasons Kit (makes 2)	$20.00		
RH160	Windsor Placemats Kit (makes 2)	$30.00		
RH170	Her Ladyship's High Tea Table Runner Kit	$42.00		
RH180	Elegance & Lace Table Runner Kit	$35.00		
RH190	Sophisticated Runner Mat Kit	$36.00		
RH195	Delicate Table Topper	$80.00		
RH200	White heavy-weight linen (sold in 1 yard increments)	$22.50		
RH210	White handkerchief linen (sold in 1 yard increments)	$25.00		
RH220	Taupe heavy-weight linen (sold in 1 yard increments)	$22.50		
RH230	Victorian Lace (Shown on pages 45) - per yard	$12.00		
RH240	Elegant Lace (Shown on page 48) - per yard	$14.00		
	Product Total			$
	Shipping & Handling (see reverse side)			$
	Tax (if California Resident — add tax for your area)			$
	Order Total			$

See reverse side for more ordering information and shipping charges.

All kits come with *everything* you need for the project:

- ✓ Fabric
- ✓ Stabilizers - as needed for the project
- ✓ 60 weight cotton sewing thread
- ✓ Embroidery thread
- ✓ Needles - sewing and pin stitching
- ✓ Lace and lace medallions*
- ✓ Double stick fusible tape*
- ✓ Gimp cord*

*if used in the project

Not included in the kits are basic sewing supplies such as pins, scissors, markers tape measures, spray adhesives, etc. Also not included are the embroidery designs because they are on the CD that come with this book.

Shipping Rates (for UPS Ground): Under $50 add $8, $51-$100 add $12, $101-$200 add $20, over $200 shipping is free.

Please send your check made out to **Sew Timeless,** with the order form to the following address:

Sew Timeless
25422 Trabuco Road, Suite 105-180
Lake Forest, CA 92630

You may also order and pay online on our web site: **www.SewTimeless.com**.